IF JESUS
HAS COME

Mark
   God bless you as
you use this book
in your ministry —
      Love
         Mom

IF JESUS
HAS COME

*BY A FORMER SKEPTIC

> THOUGHTS ON THE INCARNATION FOR SKEPTICS,
> CHRISTIANS, AND SKEPTICAL CHRISTIANS.

STEVE BROWN

A Raven's Ridge Book

BAKER BOOK HOUSE
Grand Rapids, Michigan

ISBN 0-8010-1032-2

Contents

If you don't like this book, please remember that it could have been worse were it not for the love, advice, and support of my wife, Anna, the patience of our two daughters, Robin and Jennifer, the hours of correction and typing by my administrative assistant, Cathy Wyatt, the advice of my associate, Dave O'Dowd, the encouragement and prayers of the officers, staff, and members of the Key Biscayne Presbyterian Church, and the gifted and sensitive editorial work by Larry Weeden. But then again, maybe it could have been better.

Introduction

This book is about Jesus, and I want you to know from the outset that I can hardly be called an objective observer. It would be easier for me to be an objective observer of my best friend or even my wife. When you begin to know Jesus, there is something about Him that gets under your skin. You either love Him or hate Him; you either follow Him or run from Him; you either accept His truth or reject it.

It is difficult to be neutral about Jesus. I know because I tried.

All my life I have been around a church. My father didn't care much for the church but my mother did. And what my mother decided, my brother and I accepted—we simply had no choice. On Sunday mornings we went to church. We prayed each morning before leaving for school, and we listened when Mother read the Bible.

I don't want you to get the wrong impression. My mother was not the kind of Christian who prayed on her knees on Sunday and preyed on her neighbors the rest of the week. She was (and is) a very earthy and practical follower of Christ. When my brother and I came home from school, we were never sure whom we would find at our dinner table. Mother had a way of bringing wounded people into our home. If they were hungry, they would be fed; if they needed a friend, she was their friend;

if they needed a defender, she would defend them. And she did it all for Jesus' sake. If you are ever going to be hanging over a cliff and you need someone to hold the rope, call my mother! You can be sure she won't look at the clouds or smell the flowers. She will hold the rope, for Jesus' sake.

Unfortunately, faith in Jesus is not transferable. College was a time of skepticism in my life. I was unable to run my spiritual car on my mother's gasoline. I questioned everything anyone had ever taught me; I discarded my mother's beliefs and set out to form my own. I tried to replace the "myths" of my short past with a more rational and sophisticated system that would be geared for the "real world." I got married, started working in commercial broadcasting—and registered for Boston University School of Theology.

Why, you ask, did I register for a school of theology? Because I just couldn't get away from Jesus!

Eventually I dropped out of seminary. There were financial problems and time problems. But the real reason I dropped out was that I just couldn't believe in the product. My wife was pregnant, I had a good job at a radio station in Boston, and I decided that it was time to settle down and "make an honest living."

During the months that followed, I was confused, empty, and afraid. Even the birth of our first daughter, Robin, didn't help the hurt. I walked the beaches of the South Shore on cold winter days, asking questions that had plagued me for years: What am I doing here? Does my living make any difference? Where am I going? Am I working just to make enough money to keep working?

And then the most important question: Is there a God? And if there is, what difference does it make?

Albert Camus said that the only question with which a thinking man must deal is the question of suicide. I can understand that, and there were times when it was an attractive option for me. I can remember coming home to our apartment and standing at the door and wanting to cry. I had everything I could possibly want—a wonderful wife, a beautiful new daughter, and a very good job with a great future. But it wasn't enough.

The Watcher

I went back to seminary, feeling that if there were no answers *there* . . . there were no answers.

During this whole time I felt like I was being "watched." The Watcher never spoke. He just watched silently and, though I didn't know it, lovingly. Everywhere I turned I met people who knew Him and loved Him: the afternoon disk jockey at the station; the pastor who came to record his religious program; the waitress in the coffee shop downstairs; my wife's obstetrician. They all knew the Watcher, and they talked about Him most of the time. The Watcher was Jesus, and I just couldn't get away from Him.

Don't misunderstand. I was not looking for Jesus: *He was looking for me!* He became the Watcher who was always there. I tried my best to ignore Him, but I couldn't. I tried to pretend, in my sophistication, that He didn't exist. I tried to turn away from any reality that didn't fit the reality I had created. In the fifth book of David Eddings's *Belgariad* series, General Varana, the Tolnedran, resolutely refused to believe in sorcery. He said, "It is a matter of principle, your Majesty. Tolnedrans do not believe in sorcery. I am a Tolnedran therefore I do not admit that it exists." Just at that moment a hawk landed in front of him and began to shimmer and change into a man. The narrator explains that, at that point, General Varana "resolutely turned his back and stared with apparently deep interest at the featureless hill some five miles distant."[1]

Like Varana, I refused to confront any reality that disturbed

---

1. David Eddings, *Enchanters' End Game* (New York: Ballantine Books, 1984), 202.

my comfortable skepticism. I was afraid that the Watcher really *would* be there, and that I would have to deal with Him and His demands on my life.

There were other times when I was just as afraid that He *wouldn't* be there . . . and I would have to live with the resulting meaninglessness.

Meanwhile, the Watcher watched silently.

Then our second daughter, Jennifer, was born, and in the midst of the joy and delight there was bad news. Jennifer had serious blood problems, and the doctor was afraid that one of her legs would not grow because it was not receiving proper nourishment. He said that once the blood count reached a certain level, Jennifer would be taken to Boston Children's Hospital for a complete transfusion. He mentioned the high mortality rate among children with this disorder and said, "I'm going to be perfectly honest with you, Mr. Brown. The prognosis isn't good."

A few weeks prior to Jennifer's birth, I had been introduced to some Christians who met each week for prayer, Bible study, and fellowship. I started going to those weekly meetings, not because I believed what they believed, but because it was nice to be around people who believed something. They had a warm spiritual fire, and I hovered on the cold fringes of their fire, thinking how nice it would be to be warm. The evening after Jennifer was born, I went to those dear Christians to ask for their help. I would probably have gone to a witch doctor if one had been available. But none was, so I went to the Christians.

When I walked into the group's meeting place, a number of them congratulated me on the birth of our new daughter. I don't generally talk about my problems, but that night I poured them all out. I told them how frightened and helpless I felt, and how much I loved Jennifer, even if she was only a day old.

Those dear people didn't even talk about it; they immediately started praying. They prayed for me, and for my wife, Anna, and then they prayed for Jennifer. And they prayed in the name of the Watcher, Jesus.

The next day Anna, who was still in the hospital, called me from the hospital room. She didn't say "Good morning" or "How are you?" She said, "Honey, did anybody pray last night?" I told her about the prayers that were offered the night before. She said, "The doctor came in this morning very early and said, 'This is a miracle. The blood count is normal and I am no longer worried about the leg.'"

The day Jesus made my daughter well was one of the most significant days of my life. I had friends who knew Jesus whose babies had died; I knew godly people who had never seen a miracle; I was familiar with a lot of "unanswered prayer." The question was, "Why me? Why was my prayer answered?" It certainly was not because I was good, pure, kind, or spiritual. Jesus, the Watcher, had intervened in my life in a specific and clear way, and I just couldn't understand it. Later I was to realize that Jesus does a lot of things that are hard to understand, that He reaches out to people who don't deserve it.

The day Jennifer got well was the day of beginning in my life. For the next six years I asked questions of everyone I knew who knew Jesus. I read more books than I care to remember, and I prayed to the One who watched.

"How Do You Know When You're Hooked?"

My friend Fred Smith feels that one of the problems men have today is that they never get together just to get together. So Fred often brings a group of men together for a weekend with no agenda. On one such weekend, they were meeting at a ranch in Texas. One evening the subject of God came up. Fred, who knows something about God, said that when God gets a man hooked, that man ought to give up immediately, because if he struggles, all he does is get his blood in the water. When God hooks someone, He will reel him in.

Later that night, as everyone was going back to their rooms, one man stopped Fred and asked, "Fred, how do you know when you're hooked?" Fred replied that when it happens to someone he knows it.

The next day some of the men were walking around the ranch when the man to whom Fred had spoken the night before took off his clothes and jumped into one of the ranch's water holes. It was a rather loose crowd, and no one paid any attention to the man. But at lunch that same man sat down by Fred and said, "You remember what you told me last night?" Fred replied that he did and the man went on, "Well, after I talked to you I decided I was hooked. I said to God, 'I don't want to be a preacher, but if that's what You want, I'll be a darn good one.'"

"Did you wonder what I was doing this morning when I jumped into the water hole?" he asked.

"Yes" Fred replied, "but I figured it was your business."

"Well," the man said with a grin, "I baptized myself, because if you're hooked you ought to get baptized."

After six years of asking questions, reading books, and facing doubts, I was hooked. I knelt down by the desk in my study and said, "I don't know everything about You, but I know enough to want to know You better. I'm not much, but I'm Yours. Do what You will with my life."

He did, and my life has never been the same.

That experience was a long time ago. Writing now it seems as though I'm talking about someone else. As I look back over the years, a lot of events aren't clear, but running through all of them is the reality of the love and presence of Jesus. Lots of folks have lied to me, but He has never lied, not even once. A lot of people have failed me, and I have failed a lot of people, but He has never failed, not even once. I have never had to apologize for Him or criticize Him or be ashamed of Him.

Jesus got under my skin and I can't get away from Him. Everywhere I turn, if I am quiet enough, I can hear the soft sound of His feet.

A friend declared recently that he is an atheist. He has

served as a pastor and a seminary teacher. He is the kind of person one does not expect to turn away from the faith. But he has. The interesting thing about my friend is that he denies God and the Bible and the church—but he can't bring himself to deny Jesus. When you ask him about Jesus he becomes strangely silent. I can understand that. I can understand it because I know how Jesus gets under your skin. It's sort of like a husband who has left his wife but remembers how loving and faithful she was. Whenever her name comes up in conversation, he changes the subject or grows silent. It's hard to get away from someone who loves you. Jesus' love is like that.

So don't expect me to be objective about Jesus. If I could, I would, but I can't. And to be perfectly honest with you, I don't know how *anyone* can be objective about Jesus. He doesn't allow objectivity. He forces Himself to be the issue, and then He calls for decision. In Matthew 16, there is a discussion between Jesus and His disciples. Jesus asked His disciples what people were saying about Him. They gave Jesus a number of answers. Then Jesus said, "But who do you say that I am?" (verse 15)

Jesus is still going around asking that question. I have answered that question for myself. My hope is that this book will help you find an answer for yourself. Anyway, after you read what follows, you won't be able to say, "Nobody ever told me."

One

If Jesus has come . . .
I've Heard From God

If Jesus has come . . .
I've Heard From God

God, after He spoke long ago to the fathers in the prophets in many portions and in many ways, in these last days has spoken to us in His Son. (Hebrews 1:1–2)

When I became a Christian, the act was almost totally an intellectual decision. I searched for truth, found truth, and acted accordingly. Until recently, the Christian faith has not been for me anything that had much to do with my heart. I was faithful to Christ, not because it made me feel good or because I felt close to God, but because I had decided that the Christian faith was true.

Now you must understand that there is nothing wrong with being faithful to Christ because you believe in Him intellectually. Indeed I believe that most Christians could use a little more fact and a little less feeling. Sometimes it's hard to separate religious experience from an overactive endocrine gland. You may have heard that old saying about marriage: "Kissin' don't last but cookin' do." Likewise in a genuine walk with God, feeling sometimes doesn't last when the truth does.

Nonetheless, after years of following the truth simply because it is true, I came to realize that the Christian faith must be more than just facts. I heard my brothers and sisters in

Christ talking about how Christ was "real" to them, and how they had experienced His presence in some very clear and deep ways. Listening to them, I knew that something was missing in my life. I knew a lot about God. I had read hundreds of books about Him. I knew the Bible and loved its great truths. But something was still missing. Sure, there had been those rare occasions when I had experienced God in a significant way. There had been those times when my prayer life had reality to it. And there had been those times when I was stirred emotionally. However, those experiences were few and far between. Most of the time, God seemed to have gone away on vacation to Bermuda and left me to do all His work.

I had gone too far with God to get out; leaving Him was simply not an option. I remember a Methodist minister friend who, after we had spent many hours together discussing the reliability of the Bible, decided he was going to do something about the truth he had discovered. He decided to have a series of evangelistic services in his church. He invited a well-known evangelist and advertised throughout the city. He was excited about what was going to happen.

I talked to him after the first service and asked how it had gone. He said, "Steve, not one person came! Not one! The speaker and I just went out to dinner together."

Later my friend had a series of bad physical experiences that seemed like heart attacks. Each time he was taken to the emergency room of the hospital and was told the doctors could find nothing physically wrong with him. He stopped by my study one day, and as soon as the door was closed he started to weep. He said, "I wish I could get out of this. I wish I had never learned the truths of God, but I have gone too far and seen too much to get out."

I understood his problem. In fact, it was my problem too. So I prayed, "God, You know that I have gone too far to get out, so this isn't a threat. Whether You answer yes or no to this prayer, I'll still be Your man. I'll still teach Your Word, and I'll still follow Your ways. But Father, I'm tired of just knowing about You, talking about You, and teaching about You. I want to know *You*, and I want to pay whatever price that will cost. Father, I'm so tired of hearsay. Come and reveal Yourself to me. That will be enough."

I would like to tell you that right after that prayer I heard a voice from heaven, saw a vision, or experienced a powerful manifestation of God's Spirit. I would like to say that there was a "second work of grace," or that I was given a great spiritual gift. I would like to say that but can't—because it didn't happen.

Let me tell you what did happen. God began to work in a subtle way in my life. I began taking more time just to be quiet before Him. I started reading less theology and more of the great devotional classics. I began doing less of what a friend calls "blithering" before God, and started listening and worshiping and adoring instead. And slowly I have found the Father answering my prayer that I might know Him. For the first time in my life I am able now and then to say, "This morning I was with the Father." The Bible has become more alive than ever before. Even my theology books have become more than just systems of doctrine: They are descriptions of the One I know and love.

It is one thing to know the truth about someone. It is quite another thing to know the person to whom the truth refers. I love the story of Simeon. You will find it in the second chapter of the Gospel according to Luke. Simeon served in the temple in Jerusalem. God had told him that he would see the Messiah before he died. Simeon knew the truth about God, and he understood the prophecy about the coming Messiah. He had walked in God's ways all his life, and he was familiar with God's Word. But Simeon was promised he would see for himself.

When Mary and Joseph brought the infant Jesus to the temple for circumcision, Simeon took the little baby in his arms and he knew that God had fulfilled His promise. God had allowed all his hopes to become reality. Simeon's song is one of the most beautiful in the Bible:

> Now Lord, Thou dost let Thy bondservant depart in peace, according to Thy word; for my eyes have seen Thy salvation, which Thou hast prepared in the presence of all peoples, a light of revelation to the Gentiles, and the glory of Thy people Israel. (Luke 2:29–32)

In other words, "Lord, I have seen the reality! Now You can take me home." Simeon knew the truth about God; he knew the Scriptures; he knew prophecy. But finally, he had touched the reality. He had touched the very Son of God. I can understand Simeon, having asked for the same thing from God. I knew the truth about God, but wanted to know Him myself. That hope is becoming a reality in my life. Is it changing my theology? No. Is it causing me to think differently about God? No. Have I been surprised by the new things I've learned? No. But to know the One I have worshiped and followed for so long is a whole lot better than simply knowing about Him.

God's Self-Revelation

I have said all of the above to introduce the most important and exciting fact of history: The incarnation of God in the man Jesus Christ. The Scripture says, "God was in Christ reconciling the world to Himself" (2 Cor. 5:19). God has come and revealed Himself to us, by actually entering the time and space of our world.

For thousands of years, mortals looked into the heavens and wondered: Is there a God? And if there is a God, what is He like? Is He a monster demanding the sacrifice of my children? Is He a God who started the machinery of the universe and then just walked away and left it to run on its own? Is He a God of love and compassion, or is He a God who has turned His back? Does He care?

And then the bottom-line question: "Does He care about me?"

Even long before the time of Christ there were many great men who spoke the truth about God. Abraham made a covenant with God and told others about it. Moses said that God was the great "I am." And he was right. Joshua convinced the people of God that God would make them victorious in battle. And he did. David wrote poetry about God, and the poetry was more than just words; the poetry was truth. The prophets spoke about the God who commands and judges and loves. They were right, too. A lot of people knew about God, and their information was accurate. The problem was that mere information is never enough to satisfy the human heart.

And then God, the God about whom so many had spoken, spoke. God entered time and space, and the world would never be the same. "In the beginning was the Word." (Lots of folks knew that.) "And the Word was with God." (Interesting and true theology.) *"And the Word became flesh and dwelt among us."* Now that is different! The hope became a reality; the words took on meaning; the bones took on flesh; God became a human being. God spoke, and for the first time people didn't have to ask questions and wonder. It was there for everyone to see. God had become flesh.

Now think about that! The God who created the world, who sustains the world and who controls its destiny—*that* God became a human being! The omnipotent, omnipresent, omniscient God came to a finite world. He became vulnerable to His creation. He became a human being.

A friend was at a party where a professor of theology had gotten a little tipsy. The professor leaned over to my friend and said, "You know, I really don't believe that all the things I teach are true."

My friend, a theological scholar whose intellect has not

blinded him to the truth, smiled and answered, "Yes, I know you don't believe it's true. But don't you wish it were?" The inebriated theologian, my friend said, looked as if he were going to weep. I'm convinced that a great deal of the disbelief of our time has as much to do with a fear of disappointment as with intellectual questions.

That was Thomas's problem. You'll remember that Jesus had appeared to the disciples after His death. They were excited, to say the least, that a dead man had gotten out of His grave. And the first person they reported it to was Thomas. But Thomas was a wet blanket. He said, "Unless I shall see in His hands the imprint of the nails, and put my finger into the place of the nails, and put my hand into His side, I will not believe." (John 20:25)

I can understand Thomas. He had been devastated by the death of the One he loved. He was just getting used to the idea of His death, and now someone was trying to stir up his hope. I was sitting next to a woman on a plane the other day when the subject of Christianity came up. When she learned that I was a pastor, it was clear the that conversation had come to an end. She said, "Look, Reverend, I don't want to hear what you have to say. I have been disappointed too much already. I simply can't afford to invest in hope again."

We forget our dreams. Some we forget because they are so horrible, and others we forget because they are so beautiful. On the one hand we can't stand the horror, and on the other we can't stand the hope. The good news about the incarnation is that the dream has come true. The hopes of millions have been confirmed. Reality has entered a world where men and women were afraid to hope too much lest they be disappointed too much. Beyond our wildest dreams, God has turned the fairy tale into reality. There is meaning, there is joy, there is forgiveness, there is hope, there is freedom. There is a happy ending. God has spoken! The Word has become flesh!

World History's Preparation for Jesus

If you will, allow me to give you a short history lesson. There are two great streams of human history. One is the Judeo-Christian stream. Some two thousand years before the birth of Christ, a group of nobodies in the middle of a desert came up with the crazy idea that God had chosen them to be His people. These nobodies lived in the midst of cultures far more sophisticated and civilized than their own. One would have expected that these Hebrews, with their nomadic lifestyle, would have been absorbed into the cultures that surrounded them. That is the way things happen in the "real" world. But in this case it didn't happen. In fact, just the opposite happened.

Living among people who sacrificed their children to their many gods, people who worshiped the sun and the moon, these Hebrews worshiped one God. In fact they developed the highest form of monotheism the world had ever known. Their ethical and moral value system was incredibly sophisticated, and their theology was far ahead of anything yet seen on the face of the earth. The Hebrew religion is one of the great mysteries of history. From a sociological standpoint, there is simply no explanation for its development and perseverance. From a biblical standpoint, there is no mystery at all. They really were God's people! They had been chosen. They were right.

So imagine this Judeo-Christian stream of human history, beginning in about the twentieth century B.C., moving down a corridor of time.

Now let's look at the other main stream of human history: the Greco-Roman stream. This stream began in the twelfth century B.C. with the Greek conquest of the Aegean civilization, and it moved through the Athenian golden age, the Peloponnesian War, the conquest and rule of Alexander the Great, and finally to the rule of Rome. Within this stream of human history we find our political roots. Here we find great learning, philosophy, architecture, art, and science. By the time the Romans ruled, there was a common language, a common coinage, a common road system, and best of all, peace. You may have heard the term *Pax Romana*, or "Roman Peace."

These two great streams of history moved in parallel, separate corridors of history for more than a thousand years. And here is where our history lesson becomes most interesting: In the first century, these two streams of human history crossed. And do you know what happened when they crossed? A Jew by the name of Jesus was born in a stable in Bethlehem.

From a purely human standpoint, if Jesus had been born seventy years earlier, when the Parthians occupied Jerusalem, you would never have heard His name. Nor would you have heard His name had He been born seventy years later, after the fall of Jerusalem. But during that brief interval, for the first time in human history it became possible for a story to spread throughout the Western world. For the first time in human history an idea could be heard by men and women everywhere. For the first time in human history it was possible for a man born in a little village in a small country, never traveling more than forty miles from His hometown, to become known and loved by thousands in countries and cultures far different from His own.

Do you think that was an accident? Do you think it was just one of those coincidences that happen occasionally in the annals of history? Or do you think that maybe, just maybe, God planned it all? Do you think that maybe, just maybe, all of history was prepared for this one event? Could it be that God prepared the conditions under which His coming would be the most favorable? The Bible says that, like the great communicator He is, God didn't speak until the audience became quiet. (See Rom. 5:6, Gal. 4:4.)

World Culture's Preparation for Jesus

One of the great passages in the Bible is the first eighteen
verses of the Gospel of John. The passage begins with the
words, "In the beginning was the Word." Genesis, the first book
of the Bible, begins in a similar way: "In the beginning God . . ."
I believe that John was thinking about that first beginning
in Genesis as he began his Gospel. As he thought back to Creation, another beginning came to his mind—a beginning just
as important and wonderful as the first one. In both of these
beginnings the darkness, chaos, and confusion were interrupted
by light, clarity, and consistency. In the first beginning God
began time, and in the second He made the hours count; in
the first beginning God created the process, and in the second
He gave the process meaning; in the first beginning God insti-
tuted His plan, and in the second God unveiled that plan to
humankind.

I remember when our baby daughters were brought home
from the hospital. I recall my feelings on each occasion as I
examined their tiny hands, their fragile bodies, and their beginning efforts at life. What a wondrous thing God had done!
What a great gift! What a joyous occasion! John must have felt
the same way as he looked at the universe and examined its
beginnings.

"In the beginning," says John, "was the Word." Let's think
for a moment about the word *Word.* In our culture today, we
think of words as combinations of letters and sounds that
express certain ideas. But in ancient Hebrew culture, words
were much more than that. We say, "Sticks and stones may
break my bones, but words can never hurt me." In Hebrew culture that simply was not true. In Genesis 26, for instance, Jacob
stole Esau's birthright by tricking Isaac into giving him a blessing. We say, "Big deal! What possible difference could that
make? A blessing is just words, right?" Wrong. In Hebrew culture, words had a reality all their own. Once the blessing was

uttered by Isaac, it could not be retracted. Jacob's receiving the blessing was a final reality.

Words do have power. We recognize that even in our own culture. At the end of most worship services there is benediction. A benediction is a blessing, and it is not meaningless. It is the pronouncing of words with power of blessing on a congregation.

Words have power in direct proportion to the power of the one speaking the words. Listen to what the Bible says about the power of *God's* words: "By the word of the LORD the heavens were made" (Ps. 33:6); "He sent His word and healed them, and delivered them from their destructions" (Ps. 107:20); "He sends forth His command to the earth; His word runs very swiftly" (Ps. 147:15); "So shall My word be which goes forth from My mouth; it shall not return to Me empty, without accomplishing what I desire, and without succeeding in the matter for which I sent it." (Isa. 55:11)

Now let's look at a similar concept that was developing in the other main stream of civilization. As early as 560 B.C., the Greek philosopher Heraclitus observed that the earth was changing all the time: The reason you can't go home again is that home is constantly changing, and the reason you can't step into the same river twice is that the river is constantly changing. This state of flux the Greeks observed had to be held together by something. Do you know what they said held it together? The *logos* or the "word" of God (although their definition of God was not the same as that of the Jews). The Stoics got a piece of the philosophical action, too. They said that order is brought out of chaos by (you guessed it!) the word.

All right, you ask, so what? I'll tell you so what: Note that throughout the centuries both the Jews and the Greeks were developing a concept, independently of one another, by which both cultures could understand the incarnation of Christ. God was not only preparing history, He was preparing the cultural thought forms of different civilizations to understand the coming of Christ. When John wrote, "In the beginning was the Word, and the Word was with God, and the Word was God. . . . And the Word became flesh," he was speaking a message that could be understood by everyone. The word *logos* which he used for "word" was not just Jewish or Greek or Roman. It was universal.

Do you think that was just an accident? Do you think that was just one of those interesting side roads of linguistics? Or, do you think that maybe, just maybe, God planned it all? Someone has said, "Before you criticize what I say, you should demonstrate that you understand it." Before He spoke, God made sure that the world would understand what He was going to say.

World Religions' Preparation for Jesus

Stay with me for just a little longer, and I will show you something else of great interest. We know that from earliest recorded history there has been a universal acceptance of the concept of sacrifice. All cultures about which we have information would at least agree that, "without shedding of blood there is no forgiveness" (Heb. 9:22). The ideas were primitive and unsophisticated, but the concept was the same: Sacrifice was a necessary thing to please the supreme Being, or beings.

However the concept of sacrifice was fairly undefined until the Jews came along and gave it a more specific meaning. In the biblical account of the Passover (see Ex. 12), an exciting idea began to develop. You will remember that God freed His people from Egypt by causing the death of all the first-born Egyptians throughout the land. However He allowed the Jews to escape this terrible tragedy. How? They were to sacrifice a lamb, and the blood of the lamb was to be placed around the doors of their houses.

Animal sacrifice was important throughout the religious history of Israel. And it was always recognized that those sacrifices were necessary because of sin. When we come to the New Testament, however, we find the writer of the book of Hebrews

declaring that all the sacrifices of all the Jews, and all the sacrifices of all people from all time, could not take away one single
sin: "For it is impossible for the blood of bulls and goats to take
away sins." (Heb. 10:4)

Put that thought on the back burner for just a moment while
I show you some developments in Greek thinking. More than
three centuries before the birth of Christ, Plato concluded that
the world of ordinary experience was illusory, and that the *real*
world was the world of ideas, or "forms." Everything we see and
experience, he said, is only a shadow of the real.

Plato illustrated this idea with what has been called the
"parable of the cave." In this parable, as recounted in *The Republic*, he imagined people living in a cave with an entrance open to
the light. These people had lived since birth chained to the wall
of the cave. All they could see of the outside world was the
shadows it cast on the cave wall; they never saw who or what
was making those shadows. Plato suggested that these chained
cave-dwellers would believe to be real, that which was only a
shadow. Likewise, he asserted, that which we think of as real in
our world, is only a shadow. The only true reality is the idea or
the "form" behind the things we see.

Whatever the merits of Plato's thought, his terminology
became an easy vehicle for the writer of Hebrews to explain the
connection between the age-old tradition of animal sacrifice and
Jesus Christ, the Lamb of God: "For the Law, since it has only a
shadow of the good things to come and not the very form of
things, can never by the same sacrifices year by year . . . make
perfect those who draw near" (Hebrews 10:1). The writer then
went on to show that Christ was real, whereas the other sacrifices were only shadows: "And every priest stands daily mini-
stering and offering time after time the same sacrifices, which
can never take away sins; but He, having offered one sacrifice for sins for all time, sat down at the right hand of God."
(verses 11–12)

Do you see it? God, from the beginning of recorded history, was preparing the world to understand and accept the implications of the incarnation. When John the Baptist called Jesus the "Lamb of God" (see John 1:36), he was pointing to the culmination of thousands of years of preparation, articulated by the Jews and revealed in Jesus. Peter wrote: "You were not redeemed with perishable things like silver or gold . . . but with precious blood, as of a lamb unblemished and spotless, the blood of Christ" (1 Peter 1:18–19). God had planted the idea of sacrifice within all human cultures, so that when He spoke through Christ, the world would understand. Not only that, but He also had enabled the concept of shadow and reality to explain the incarnation of Christ as the true sacrificial Lamb.

Do you think it was an accident? Do you think it was merely a coincidence? Do you think it was a game with words and ideas? If you think so, I have some swampland in Florida to sell you!

God has come to our world. History points to it; cultural thought-forms testify to its reality; even pagan religions anticipated it; and a loving, guiding, and sovereign hand prepared for it. God has spoken in Christ. He has come, so that we wouldn't have to settle for knowing about Him, but could actually know *Him*.

Paul Harvey tells the story about a man who was an atheist. His wife and children were Christians, however, and every Christmas Eve they went to church, while the man stayed at home and read the paper. When the family returned from the service, they opened their presents and celebrated the holiday.

One particular Christmas Eve, the family had gone to church as usual, and the man was reading the paper. He heard a noise coming from the living room window and he went to check. He found that a snowstorm had developed and that the birds outside, trying to escape the storm, were trying to get into the house by flying against the picture window. They saw the warmth of the house through the window, and they were flying against it and falling to the ground.

The man decided to try to help the birds. He put on his heavy coat and boots and went out into the yard. He tried to shoo the birds away from the window, but to the birds he was an enemy and they flew away from him, and right against the window. He walked down to the barn, opened the doors, and turned on the light, thinking that the birds would see the light and fly into the barn for its warmth. But as he tried to get them to see, they only flew from him, frightened by his efforts to help.

As he stood in the storm and watched the birds, the man thought to himself, *Those dumb birds. They simply don't understand. If I could just find a way to communicate with them. If I could just find a way to let them know that I am not their enemy. If—if I could only become a bird, I could make them understand.*

At that moment the bells on the church steeple began to ring, signaling the end of the Christmas Eve service. As the man heard the bells, he thought of God, whose feelings were not dissimilar to his own in trying to communicate with the birds. In a flash of understanding and insight, the man realized what Christmas was all about, and he fell on his knees in the snow and prayed, "Oh God, I just didn't understand. I just didn't understand."

That is what happened in the incarnation. The God of the universe entered time and space, so that we might understand.

For Personal Insight or Group Discussion

1. Which of the following passages from the Bible speak of knowing *about* God? Which speak of knowing *Him*, in a personal way? Which speak of both?

   Job 42:5
   Psalm 100:3
   Jeremiah 31:33–34
   Acts 17:22–31
   Romans 1:18–20
   Philippians 3:7–10

2. What do the following passages from the Psalms say about the emotional well-being that can come from knowing our Creator in a personal way?

   Psalm 1:1–3
   Psalm 23
   Psalm 27:4–5
   Psalm 84:1–4
   Psalm 91:1–2

3. What does being "reconciled" mean to you, in terms of your relationships with other people, and with God? (Review 2 Cor. 5:19–20.)

4. What does Romans 3:23 say about your need for reconciliation with God? How does verse 24 provide the answer? (See also John 3:16–17.)

5. The Bible teaches that Jesus Christ was God "incarnate," that is, in human form. "And the Word became flesh and dwelt among us" (John 1:14). What do we learn about God from the way Jesus lived His life on this earth?

6. On the basis of what you have read in this chapter, do you
   agree that Jesus was born "at the right time"? (Review Rom.
   5:6 and Gal. 4:4.) How did pre-Christian culture and religion
   prepare the way for his coming?

Two

If Jesus has come . . .
My Life Has Meaning

If Jesus has come ...
My Life Has Meaning

Whoever drinks of the water that I shall give him shall never thirst; but the water that I shall give him shall become in him a well of water springing up to eternal life. (John 4:14)

A mid-life crisis is a time when a man or woman realizes that time is limited and will run out someday. It is a time when he or she realizes that life is finite and that the goals that were a part of youthful dreaming are probably not going to be reached. It is a time of transition between doing and thinking, between asking how and asking why, between moving from birth and moving toward death.

Just a few years ago I began my mid-life crisis. I didn't really know you called it that until some friends purchased a Christian bookstore, and invited me to come and see it. As I was browsing through the shelves of books in the store, my friend reached to a shelf just above where I was standing and said, "Oh, Steve, I have the perfect book for you." She handed me a book dealing with mid-life crisis and its attendant problems. I suspect I looked rather abashed because my friend, who is quick on the uptake, said, "Oh, I don't mean it's for you; I mean it will be helpful in your counseling."

After reading the book, I finally had a name for an ailment from which I had suffered most of my life. There is something about putting a name to a problem that makes one feel better about it. Of course, I had not solved the problem, but I had a name: "mid-life crisis." I began to share my newly named problem, and, "a funny thing happened to me on the way to the forum." I found that almost every thinking person I knew was going through a mid-life crisis, and some of them weren't even in mid-life!

I also found that mid-life crisis is an ancient disease. The psalmist described the symptoms quite adequately:

Hear my prayer, O LORD!
And let my cry for help come to Thee.
Do not hide Thy face from me in the day of my distress;
Incline Thine ear to me;
In the day when I call answer me quickly.
For my days have been consumed in smoke,
And my bones have been scorched like a hearth.
My heart has been smitten like grass and has withered away.
Indeed, I forget to eat my bread.
Because of the loudness of my groaning
My bones cling to my flesh.
I resemble a pelican of the wilderness;
I have become like an owl of the waste places.
I lie awake,
I have become like a lonely bird on a housetop.
(Ps. 102:1–7)

A mid-life crisis is, of course, not a *mid-life* crisis at all. It is just a crisis of meaning, and most of us do everything in our power to keep from going through such a crisis. We sterilize everything from birth to death. We avoid any conversation that goes beyond the baseball scores. We ease the pain with drugs or booze. We turn away from every tragedy and hide from every hurt. We take every trauma and make a sit-com out of it. We cover every flaw with vitamins and make-up. We operate under the ancient principle that if we don't think about something, maybe it will go away.

One of the things I have noticed after many years of dealing with terminally ill people is that friends and family members usually don't know what to say to the dying, so they don't say anything. Even doctors and nurses avoid going into the rooms of dying patients, because they don't know what to do, and the death of a patient reminds them of their own eventual death.

A few months ago I was on a plane from Miami to Los Angeles. When the plane took off, the people in my section were, as I remember it, more boisterous than the general run of airline passengers. There was a group of six or eight young men who were going home after a business meeting in Miami. They were talking about what they were going to do when they got home and how much fun they had had away from home. Two teenage girls in front of me talked about boys. Among the passengers in this section was the usual mix of tired salespeople trying to sleep, parents trying to calm their children, and people, like me, making plans for whatever was going to happen in Los Angeles.

Then a woman screamed. It was not a moderate scream, either; it was bloodcurdling. She turned to the quickly approaching flight attendant and said through her sobs, "My daughter is dying!" For the next twenty minutes, three physicians culled from the passengers worked frantically on the teenage girl, who slowly died in the aisle beside my seat. The pilot made an emergency landing in Dallas, and the sheet-draped body of the girl was taken off the plane accompanied by the sobbing mother.

I'm no stranger to death. No pastor is. I have stood by more deathbeds than I can count and have cleaned up after more suicides than I care to remember. So I was able to be rather objective about the tragic scene taking place on the airplane that day. While not personally unmoved, I was simply able to sit back

and observe the reactions of those around me. There was a
strange, eerie silence on the rest of the trip to Los Angeles. The
teenagers who had been talking about boys before were silently
crying and embracing each other. The tired salespeople were no
longer sleeping. And the men returning from their convention
were trying to forget the scene they had just witnessed by con-
suming as many of the free drinks offered by the airline as they
could get down. No one spoke, as each person on that airplane
contemplated his or her own thoughts about tragedy and death.

Most of the time we can escape such thoughts. When we see
death, we can turn away. But we were on an airplane, and nobody could leave. It was an interesting "controlled" experiment.

I had a strange desire to stand up and preach a sermon. Of
course that was not possible; but had it been, I can assure you I
would have had a most attentive audience. In fact, a crisis is
sometimes the best time to get people to listen to truth. If I
could have preached a sermon that day, it would have included
what I'm going to tell you in this chapter.

The Lessons of Ecclesiastes

Ecclesiastes is one of my favorite books in the Bible. The
writer of Ecclesiastes was an ancient Albert Camus, articulating
the emptiness and meaninglessness of a world where God is the
only hope. Listen to what he said:

> What advantage does man have in all his work
> Which he does under the sun?
> A generation goes and a generation comes,
> But the earth remains forever.
> Also, the sun rises and the sun sets;
> And hastening to its place it rises there again.
> Blowing toward the south,
> Then turning toward the north,

The wind continues swirling along;
And on its circular courses the wind returns.
All the rivers flow into the sea,
Yet the sea is not full.
To the place where the rivers flow,
There they flow again.
All things are wearisome;
Man is not able to tell it.
The eye is not satisfied with seeing,
Nor is the ear filled with hearing.
That which has been is that which will be,
And that which has been done is that which will be done.
So, there is nothing new under the sun. (1:3–9)

I, the Preacher, have been king over Israel in Jerusalem. And I set my mind to seek and explore by wisdom concerning all that has been done under heaven. It is a grievous task which God has given to the sons of men to be afflicted with. I have seen all the works which have been done under the sun, and behold, all is vanity and striving after wind. What is crooked cannot be straightened, and what is lacking cannot be counted. I said to myself, "Behold, I have magnified and increased wisdom more than all who were over Jerusalem before me; and my mind has observed a wealth of wisdom and knowledge." And I set my mind to know wisdom and to know madness and folly; I realized that this also is striving after wind. Because in much wisdom there is much grief, and increasing knowledge results in increasing pain. (verses 12–18)

And then after showing the emptiness of life, the Preacher said, "Remember Him [God] before the silver cord is broken and the golden bowl is crushed, the pitcher by the well is shattered and the wheel at the cistern is crushed; then the dust will return to the earth as it was, and the spirit will return to God who gave it. 'Vanity of vanities,' says the Preacher, 'all is vanity!'" (12:6–8)

Do you ever wonder why you keep doing the things you do? Do you sometimes get to feeling that you get up every morning and go to work, in order to make enough money to pay the mortgage and buy the food . . . just so that you'll have a place to sleep and eat in order to get up in the morning and go to work!

There's a great little book by Trina Paulus titled *Hope for the Flowers*. It is a picture book for adults similar to the Dr. Seuss books for children. The story traces the life of a caterpillar named Stripe, from birth to butterfly. Soon after birth, Stripe began trying to decide what to do with his life. He met a girl caterpillar named Yellow, and for a while their relationship was enough to sustain Stripe. But eventually he began to wonder if there was something more to life.

One day Stripe noticed a gigantic pillar, and on closer examination he realized it was a pillar of *caterpillars*, stretching up into the sky. As he looked closer he noted that the caterpillars were climbing over one another, trying to get to the top of the pillar. And so Stripe began to climb too:

> Stripe didn't seem just "disciplined" to others—he seemed ruthless. Even among climbers he was special. He didn't think he was against anybody. He was just doing what he had to if he was to get to the top. "Don't blame me if you don't succeed! It's a tough life. Just make up your mind," he would have said had any caterpillar complained.[1]

It was difficult, but finally Stripe made it almost to the top of the pillar of caterpillars. He found that no matter how hard he tried, he couldn't get any higher. Then he heard someone above him say there was no way to get higher without getting rid of "them." And then the pillar began to shake and caterpillars began to scream and fall. Then there was silence:

---

1. Trina Paulus, *Hope for the Flowers* (Paramus, N .J .: Paulist Press, 1972), 89.

Frustration surged through Stripe. But as he was agreeing this was the only way up he heard a tiny whisper from the top: "There's nothing here at all!" It was answered by another: "Quiet fool! They'll hear you down the pillar. We're where they want to get. That's what's here!"

Stripe felt frozen. To be so high and not high at all! It only looked good from the bottom. The whisper came again. "Look over there—another pillar—and there too—everywhere!" Stripe became angry as well as frustrated. 'My pillar' he moaned, 'only one of thousands. Millions of caterpillars climbing nowhere! Something is really wrong but . . . what else is there?'"[2]

In Stripe's final question we see the anxiety of mid-life crisis, adolescence crisis, and old-age crisis. What is life all about? Is this all there is? Is there something more than this pillar?

Now let's return to the book of Ecclesiastes. In fact I suggest you stop reading right here, turn to Ecclesiastes, and read the whole book! It's a short book, and well worth your time. But reading it makes a question simmer in the back of your mind: Why would God allow a book that seems so cynical and nihilistic to be in His revelation? I suspect there are five good reasons, and all of them must be understood before we turn to how the incarnation of Christ answers the problem of human meaninglessness.

First, God allowed Ecclesiastes to be included because it strikes to the very heart of the easy sentimentality and superficiality that so often plagues the people of God. Somehow Christians have adopted the idea that the world is the playground for God's people, a place where God's main business is to make His people happy.

President Robinson of Middlebury College once told a graduating class, "You may have thought, having finished your finals

---

2. Ibid., 94.

and having turned in your last papers, that you now can see the light at the end of the tunnel. Well, dear friends, if you can see the light at the end of the tunnel, you are probably facing the wrong direction." Although it is cynical, that is good advice about the way the world really is. As a matter of fact, this world has sorrow, hurt, tragedy, and sickness. I don't like that any more than you do, but it is true nonetheless.

Every once in a while someone asks me, "Pastor, are you happy?" Well, sometimes I'm happy and sometimes I'm not, but the question itself is irrelevant. God didn't put us in this world to be happy. That is where "prosperity theology" has made a great mistake. Faithful, consistent Christians do suffer. So either God is a monster and a liar or some of His teachers got their wires crossed. Don't believe anybody who tells you that it is always God's will for Christians to be healthy, wealthy, and wise. It didn't happen to Jesus, or to Paul, or to Peter. It probably won't happen to us, either. The book of Ecclesiastes reminds us that the way to meaning is not through seeking a dream world that doesn't exist.

Second, God allowed the book of Ecclesiastes to be included in the canon of Scripture because it allows the believer to benefit from someone else's experience, someone who was extremely honest and wise. Have you ever been tempted to return to the world's ways in order to be happy? There are those times when I sit in my study after a day of listening to the hurt of my people, tired from trying to be faithful, tired from trying to be a teacher of things that are hard to understand and even harder to live. On those occasions I can empathize a little with the prophet Jeremiah.

Jeremiah was the least successful man of God who ever lived. Everything he tried, failed; every time he told God's people to do one thing, they did another; every time he was faithful, everybody else seemed unfaithful. The people he was sent to serve tried to kill him. Finally, Jeremiah asked the Lord, "Why has the way of the wicked prospered? Why are all those who deal in treachery at ease? Thou hast planted them, they have also taken root; they grow, they have even produced fruit." (Jer. 12:1–2)

I can understand Jeremiah, and I'll bet you can, too. Sometimes the struggle just doesn't seem worth it. Well, when I start feeling that way, I turn to the book of Ecclesiastes, where we see how empty and banal the way of the world really is. Then the world isn't so attractive, and I think, "I don't need that. There's no meaning there."

A third probable reason God gave us Ecclesiastes is that it enables us to deal with the ambiguity of life, with the fact that life appears simple but does not have simple answers. It helps us to see how important it is not to take life too seriously. I have a friend who says that in order to be a Christian in this world, one must have a tolerance for ambiguity. In other words, if we are to look for meaning, we must be very careful not to look for it in life.

Have you ever noticed how Christians like systems? I used to preach a sermon on, "The Five Ways to Know God's Will." A few years ago I was trying to discover God's will in a particular area of my life, and I went through all five of those ways and still didn't know God's will! Trying to find meaning in systems can be devastating. You will find systems everywhere: The Four Steps to Salvation; How to Find Peace; Ten Rules for Parents; How to Save Your Marriage.

Don't get me wrong. I'm not saying there isn't truth in such systems. I'm simply saying that life doesn't fit into a neat, nice, compact system. If it did, there would be no problem finding life's meaning. The writer of Ecclesiastes said that life is filled with ambiguity, and that if you try to find your meaning by the resolution of the ambiguity, you are going to be disappointed.

A fourth reason for the book of Ecclesiastes is that it provides a warning for those who would reduce the Scriptures to humanistic secularism. Every once in a while, someone says to me about a friend, "He is a Christian, but he doesn't believe in God." What he is telling me is that so and so is a "good person."

But the writer of Ecclesiastes says that a very good person and a very bad person face the same fate: meaninglessness.

Somehow we have believed the myth that, "Goodness is its own reward." Let me tell you something important: Goodness is *not* its own reward. In fact, goodness is stupid if one is good without reference to God. Mark Twain said that the church is a place where a nice, respectable person stands in front of other nice, respectable people and urges them to be nicer and more respectable. If that is all the church does, it is leading people down the wrong path. There is no meaning in mere goodness. Besides, how do we know that what we call good is really good?

Finally, the book of Ecclesiastes is included in God's book because it forces believers to the only source of meaning, God the Father. It is said that Alexander the Great once found an enemy soldier dying of cold and exposure. He had his servants bring the soldier into his tent and put him on his own bed until he was warm. When the man woke and noticed that he was in the king's bed, he became frightened. Alexander smiled and said, "To recline in the bed of the Macedonian king is death, but to recline in my bed is life." The writer of Ecclesiastes, in twelve chapters, pulled the slats out of all royal beds save One. He said, "The conclusion, when all has been heard, is: fear God and keep His commandments, because this applies to every person." (Eccl. 12:13)

John the Baptist's Example

In Luke's Gospel we read about a man who was searching for meaning. His name was John the Baptist, and he needed to know the truth because he was going to die and he was afraid his death would prove to be meaningless.

John was born to a priest named Zacharias and his God-fearing wife, Elizabeth, and he was consecrated in his mother's womb to be a servant of God. As a young man, John went into the wilderness to begin the ministry God had given him. If you had known John you might not have liked him. He was not a good-old-boy-back-slapper; he was a lightning bolt in the hand of the Almighty. He dressed in camel hair, ate wild locusts, and was very earthy and direct. His message was twofold: 1) you are sinners; and, 2) you must repent and be baptized. But more important than even that message was the fact that John was to prepare the way for the coming Messiah. In fact, John identified Jesus as the Messiah.

In Luke 7, John was awaiting execution by Herod because he had challenged the king's immorality. The pathos of the situation is almost overwhelming. John knew he was going to die, but he didn't fear death. He feared instead that his life had been lived in vain. He feared that Jesus wasn't the Messiah after all. John's problem was not death, but meaninglessness.

One of my favorite books is *Prayers*, by Michel Quoist, a French priest. It contains some of the most beautiful and honest prayers I have ever read. Let me quote just a few lines from one of those prayers, "It Is Dark," which reflect the despair John the Baptist must have felt in his final hours.

> Lord, it is dark.
> Lord, are you here in my darkness? . . .
> You have taken me far, Lord; trusting, I followed you, and you
>   walked at my side,
> And now, in the middle of the desert, at night, suddenly you
>   have disappeared.
> I call, and you do not answer.
> I search, and I do not find you.
> I have left everything, and now am left alone.
> Your absence is my suffering.
>
> Lord, it is dark.
> Lord, are you here in my darkness?

Where are you, Lord?
Do you love me still?
Or have I wearied you?
Lord, answer, Answer!

It is dark.[3]

In his despair, John the Baptist did the only thing he knew to do: He sent his disciples to Jesus with a list of questions—halting, hurting, helpless questions. "Jesus," they said, "John wants to know . . . he is afraid, lonely, and facing death. John wants to know about You. Are You the Messiah, or should we go and search out another? Has John wasted his life and his ministry?"

Perhaps you have had your periods of doubt and fear, too. Perhaps you have wondered if life has meaning and have asked the same questions John asked. Jesus is still giving the answer He gave to John's crisis of meaning. He gave John meaning, and can give you meaning, with a demonstration, an exhortation, a commendation, and a declaration.

Jesus' Demonstration

Jesus' demonstration, in answer to John's questions, was this: "Go and report to John what you have seen and heard: the blind receive sight, the lame walk, the lepers are cleansed, and the deaf hear, the dead are raised up, the poor have the gospel preached to them" (Luke 7:22). *If Jesus has come, there is meaning in life because in His coming and in His loving there is a demonstration of God's care for His people.* If nothing more, the incarnation is the way the infinite breaks into the finite, to demonstrate in time and space that there is meaning. If there is no God, there is no value; if there is no value, there is no meaning; if there is no

---

3. Michel Quoist, *Prayers* (New York: Sheed and Ward, 1963), 139–140.

meaning, then you are a turnip! But there is meaning, because God has come and has demonstrated His love for us.

He is still demonstrating His love for us in Christ. Not too long ago I was having my weekly pity party, feeling that my ministry was of little or no use to anyone. And then came a long distance call from a Methodist minister in another state. He said, "Steve, you don't know me, but the Baptist minister in our town gave me some of your tapes. I would like to be placed on the Key Life Tape list, but, more than that, I wanted you to know that Jesus speaks through you, and I'm glad."

It was almost as if Jesus was saying to the angels, "Go tell Steve that the hungry are fed."

Last week I thought the world had come to an end. All my plans looked like Jericho after the trumpets; I had been criticized for an action that was well-intentioned; a letter came that was very critical of something I had written; one of my close friends had left the ministry and declared his atheism; and a man had left our church angry about something I had said. I was at the point where you say, "What's the use?" And then I opened a letter that had been on my desk all morning. It was from a dear Christian brother. He wrote, "Steve, I was praying for you this morning, and Jesus told me to write. Well, maybe that is a little too spiritual, but I did feel 'led' to write. I wanted you to know that I love you and the way God uses you in my life." And between the lines I saw once again the message from Jesus, "Go tell Steve he's not alone."

I have been walking with Jesus for a long time, and He has always found such ways to demonstrate His love for me. Sometimes He demonstrates His love through compassion in one of His friends. At other times His demonstration is a direct answer to a prayer. And sometimes His demonstration is in the simple form of a loving listener. There are times when my only comfort is Jesus Himself, and in those times I realize a truth from Ron Dunn: "A lot of people say, 'Jesus is all I need.' You will never know if Jesus is all you need, until Jesus is all you've got. When

Jesus is all you've got, then you will know that Jesus is all you need."

It began in the incarnation. We don't find platitudes there or empty religious language. We asked God: Are you there? Do you love? How much do you love? And Jesus said, "I love you this much." And He stretched out His arms on a cross and died. That was the beginning of a pattern, a pattern that points to a God who is really there. If Jesus has come, there really is a God; if there really is a God, there is value; if there is value, there is meaning; and if there is meaning, I can keep on keeping on.

Jesus' Exhortation

Jesus continued His answer to John's messengers with an exhortation. He called on John, rather than despairing over his unanswered questions, to build on what he knew: "And blessed is he who keeps from stumbling over Me" (Luke 7:23).

To understand what Jesus was saying, we must remember two things: First, John was a man who knew the Scripture; and second, John used the title "Messiah" based upon his knowledge of the Scripture. He meant by "Messiah" a great political leader who would restore Israel to her place among the nations, restore righteousness on the earth, and restore respect for the name of God in the world. So you can imagine why he was confused. He had expected someone quite different from Jesus. He had expected a political and military figure, a great charismatic leader. But Jesus was none of those things, and it shook John to the foundations of his faith and sense of meaning.

Of course there are actually *two* themes running through the messianic prophecies in the Old Testament. One deals with the "suffering servant," the other with the political and military leader. We know that Jesus has already fulfilled the first in the incarnation, and that He will fulfill the second upon His triumphant return. But John didn't know that, and thus his dilemma.

When Jesus told John's disciples to report what they had seen, He was saying, "John, please know that I *am* the Messiah, but that I am fulfilling only half of the messianic prophecies. Your questions will have to wait, but I have answered enough of them to let you know that you haven't missed the road. Blessed is the person who doesn't take offense at ("stumble over") Me."

Christ's exhortation to John as he faced meaninglessness was, "Don't try to figure everything out; you already have enough information to know the truth." Someone came to me recently and said, "Steve, it must be wonderful to be a Bible teacher and to have the answers." I didn't tell my friend the whole truth then, because he was a new Christian and he wasn't ready to hear it; but the truth is this: The more I walk with Jesus, the less sure I am of a lot of things—and the more sure I am of *Him.*

Let me give you a principle that will help you when you're confused: Whatever you think God is doing in your life right now, He probably isn't. That principle helps me live with the paradox of trying to put God in a box. You see, He wants us to learn to trust Him no matter what happens. Meaning isn't to be found in having all questions answered, all problems solved, all ambiguity resolved. Meaning is found only in the fact that Jesus has come. If that is true, then the rest will be okay.

Jesus' Commendation

Having demonstrated His messiahship, and having exhorted John to be encouraged by that demonstration, Jesus then commended John to his messengers: "But what did you go out to see? A prophet? Yes, I say to you, and one who is more than a prophet. This is the one about whom it is written, 'Behold, I send My messenger before Your face, who will prepare Your way before You.' I say to you, among those born of women, there is no one greater than John" (verses 26–28). In other words, "John, as confused and frightened as you are, you're doing it right!"

Some time ago, I was having problems trying to balance my work as a pastor with my writing and my outside speaking engagements. God has blessed me with a very affirming and loving congregation of believers at Key Biscayne, who have never tried to force me into some kind of false ministerial role. My only problem was my own feelings of guilt. I decided to seek the advice of someone who had dealt successfully with the problem, so I called Stuart Briscoe. The advice he gave me was very wise and helpful. He asked me some questions and listened to the answers, and then he said, "Steve, you are doing it right, but you will probably still feel guilty." I have thought about what he said on more than one occasion when the guilt feelings have returned. I've been able to deal with the guilt because someone I respect told me that, at least in this one area, I was doing it right.

The incarnation of Christ enables us to know what the right track is, even when we don't feel very good about it. Longfellow's lines certainly don't apply to all who aspire to be role models, but if applied to the Son of God they are quite appropriate:

> Lives of great men all remind us
> We can make our lives sublime,
> And, departing, leave behind us
> Footprints on the sands of time;
> Footprints, that perhaps another,
> Sailing o'er life's solemn main,
> A forlorn and shipwrecked brother,
> Seeing, shall take heart again.[4]

The old spiritual speaks to the issue when it says, "You done showed us how." In the incarnation, Jesus showed us how; He gave us a model of following the God of the universe. He com-

---

4. Henry Wadsworth Longfellow, from the poem "A Psalm of Life" quoted in *Major American Writers*, Jones, Leisy & Ludwig, eds. (New York: Harcourt, Brace and Company, 1952), 581.

mends us when we conform to that model, and in the conformity and the affirmation there is meaning. The most meaningful words in the world come from His lips: "Well done, good and faithful slave." (Matt. 25:21)

Jesus' Declaration

Jesus concluded His response to John's messengers by saying, "For John the Baptist has come eating no bread and drinking no wine; and you say, 'He has a demon!' The Son of Man has come eating and drinking; and you say, 'Behold, a gluttonous man, and a drunkard, a friend of tax-gatherers and sinners!' Yet wisdom is vindicated by all her children" (Luke 7:33–35). Stated in the vernacular, Jesus was saying, "It will all come out in the wash!"

In Jeremiah 32, Jeremiah was called by God to purchase a field in Anathoth. That was not an unusual thing to do, but in this case the Chaldean army was preparing to invade, and the property was soon going to be worthless. Jeremiah went to a man by the name of Hanamel and asked to purchase the property. Hanamel thought Jeremiah was a fool, but Hanamel was not one to pass up a good deal even if it did come from a fool.

Jeremiah explained why he bought the property: "Thus says the LORD of hosts, the God of Israel, 'Take these deeds, this sealed deed of purchase, and this open deed, and put them in an earthenware jar, that they may last a long time.' For thus says the LORD of hosts, the God of Israel, 'Houses and fields and vineyards shall again be bought in this land.'" (Jer. 32:14–15)

History may try to vindicate the bad guys; but Jeremiah looked to the future and knew that God's people would eventually return to their land. In similar fashion, Jesus' coming declared that every act of obedience, every prayer, every bit of suffering for righteousness' sake is taken into account in God's economy. God does balance His books, and because He does, a wrong road will go to the wrong place, and a right road will go to the right place. The road always ends in the place where it leads. The ambiguity is still there, but hang tough because Jesus has promised. If He has come, then life has meaning.

Newspapers have a way of being cynical. Cynicism is sometimes needed, but I think the writers of an editorial in a Chicago paper went a bit too far: "The cheek of every American must tingle with shame as he reads the silly, dish-watery utterances of a man who has to be pointed out to intelligent foreigners as the President of the United States."

Perhaps, like John, you are sitting around wondering if there is any real meaning to your life. Perhaps you find yourself wondering if, given the hatred and the helplessness of the world, you ought to join the cynics. That is understandable. Sometimes I feel that way, too. But it isn't going to happen with me, because God has promised that all who follow Christ will shine like the sun.

John knows that now. In fact, he knew it for sure shortly after he received his message from Jesus. He was executed, and at that very second he stood in the throne room of the God of the universe. I suspect that God laughed and said, "John, I told you so."

Oh yes, that editorial from the Chicago newspaper: It was written in 1865 in the Chicago *Times*. It was in reference to Abraham Lincoln's "Gettysburg Address." Things do have a way of coming out in the wash.

For Personal Insight or Group Discussion

1. What kinds of events or circumstances can bring about a "crisis of meaning" in your life? If you have gone through such a crisis, what people, events, or beliefs helped you during that time?

2. Can you identify with what Solomon says in Ecclesiastes? Are the issues he faced at all similar to the issues you face, nearly 3000 years later? Can you accept the answer he gives, in chapter 12?

3. Can you identify with Stripe the caterpillar? Have you known people who are like Stripe? What does the Bible have to say to such people?

4. Do you agree with the statement that, "If we are to look for meaning, we must be very careful not to look for it in life"? How might the following Bible authors respond to that question?

      Solomon (Eccl. 12:13.)   John (1 John 2:15–17)
      David (Ps. 84:1–4, 10)   Paul (Phil. 3:8–11.)
      Joshua (Josh. 24:14–15)

5. What "demonstration" did Jesus give in answer to John the Baptist's questions about Him? (Luke 7:21-22.) Have you seen similar demonstrations of His love in your own life?

6. Are there people in your life who have left "Footprints on the sands of time"—that is, who have left a good example for you to follow? What kind of "footprints" are you leaving? How can this be a part of finding meaning in your life?

Three

If Jesus has come . . .
Satan Has Lost

If Jesus has come...
Satan Has Lost

The Son of God appeared for this purpose, that He might destroy the works of the devil. (1 John 3:8)

If you are typical, you will react to this chapter in one of two ways: Either you will find it most fascinating, or you will laugh it off as the silly musings of an outdated religionist. Those two reactions represent the two great dangers into which Christians can fall when dealing with the subject of Satan.

There was a time in my life when I was tempted by the second of those extremes. I simply couldn't bring myself to believe that there could be personal evil in the world, far less that it was a person called Satan. You see, I was an intellectual, and intellectuals are far too sophisticated to hold some medieval view of a wicked man running around in a weird, red suit carrying a pitchfork. Oh yes, I delighted in discussing Goethe's *Faust*. We intellectuals could deal with the character of Mephistopheles without sacrificing our intellectual credibility. Dante's Lucifer and Milton's Satan, by far the most attractive characters in *The Inferno* and *Paradise Lost*, were safe; but to discuss a real, live devil was simply beyond consideration.

Sometimes when I need to be humbled before God, I reread

some of the sermons I preached right after graduating from seminary. The sermons make me blush. The people in the first
church I served were very forgiving of their young pastor, but
there are many times I wish I could go back to that little church
on Cape Cod and apologize for some of the things I taught those
dear people.

There is one sermon in particular that I sometimes reread. I
was just out of seminary and was preaching on the temptations
of Jesus. As you know, Satan is a prominent figure in the
accounts of Jesus' temptations. In that sermon I had great diffi-
culty referring to him as "Satan" or the "devil." So, do you know
what I did? Whenever it became necessary to refer to Satan, I
called him the "metaphorical personification of evil."

One time Albert Schweitzer was doing some manual labor
at his hospital at Lambarene. A native was watching, and
Schweitzer asked him to help. The native refused, saying that
he was not a common laborer but an intellectual. Schweitzer
turned back to his work, saying, "Once I thought I was an intellectual, too." Well, once I thought I was an intellectual, and that
thought prevented me from seeing a lot of truths, among them
the reality, personality, and power of Satan.

There is the other extreme of seeing Satan around every cor-
ner and under every bed. Probably at no time in the history of
the church has so much been written about Satan. A lot of the
literature is helpful, but much of it is plain silly. With the pub-
licity Satan has been getting lately, some folks have gone "Satan
happy." Satan and his demons are everywhere. If you sin, the
devil made you do it. If you are angry, you have a "spirit" of
anger. And if you can't quit smoking, your problem isn't that
you lack discipline; your problem is that you have a demon of
addiction.

In a congregation I once served, there developed a fascina-
tion with demons and demonology, and one Sunday morning I
left my notes (pastors often get into trouble when they leave
their notes) to speak to the issue. Among other things, I said,

"Some of you are so fascinated by Satan that you have taken your eyes off God, and a lot of your frustration is nothing more or less than silly superstition. One of these days some of you are going to meet a real demon, and it is going to scare your socks off." I was told later that some people were angry at me, and one couple walked out of the church never to return. I wish the couple had come back to the church because my remarks were not as loving as they ought to have been, but what I said needed to be heard. Satan gets a lot of mileage out of the Christian's fear, and it is from gasoline for which he didn't pay. Rumors of Satan's power are far greater than its reality, and it is time Christians realized that.

It is said that Samuel Rutherford, the seventeenth-century Scottish clergyman, once heard a noise in his sitting room. It was the middle of the night, and Rutherford decided to check it out. He climbed out of bed and went to the sitting room. He found Satan, as big as life, sitting in his favorite chair. Rutherford laughed and said, "Oh, it's only you," and went back to bed to sleep.

In the next few pages I have some bad news and some good news for you. The bad news is that Satan is very real and he is out to get you. The good news is that because Jesus has come, Satan is a defeated foe. As someone has said, "The dragon has been slain, but his tail still swishes." Let's look at the bad news first.

The Reality of Satan

There is a devil and I have seen him. I have seen him walking down the streets of a city slum; I have watched him do his work with a needle dripping heroin; I have seen him in a bottle clutched in the hand of a drunk asleep on a bench on Boston Common. I have seen Satan's handwriting in a suicide note, and have noticed his smile as crowds lined up to watch an "adult" movie. I have seen the work of Satan in a crushed automobile, an empty stomach, and a dead soldier. I have seen Satan in the words of a man who said he didn't need God and in the sneer of a woman who was asked if she knew Christ. I have seen Satan in the hurt, emptiness, and frustration of humanity. Sometimes I see him in my own doubts, depression, lust, anger, and fear.

The writers of the Bible didn't hesitate to talk about Satan. They called him the liar, the accuser, the dragon, the serpent, and the ruler of the world. What the Bible says about the work of Satan is enough to make any believer pause. Satan is the tempter who would lure the believer away from the walk of faith. He seeks to destroy God's Word in the experience of the believer. He is an accuser who would cripple the Christian with guilt and fear. He sometimes becomes dominant in an individual life either in person or through one of his minions. Satan is responsible for sin and unbelief, and he rejoices whenever he can turn anyone away from the truth. He would have you fall down and worship him even if you call him by another name. He is real; he is alive; and he is dangerous.

Marshall Fishwick wrote in *Faust Revisited*, "There are those today who do not believe in the Devil. They are the first fallen: for Satan always begins by trying to convince us that he doesn't exist. The wisest human minds, and the God made Man, have acknowledged the existence of the forces of evil, and wrestled with them. So must we."[1]

If you are having trouble believing in the reality of the devil, let me say a couple of things to you. First, truth and reality have an uncomfortable tendency to defy both systems and convention. The intelligent searcher after truth will not limit himself by his own presuppositions. Don't let your preconceived ideas of Satan and those who believe in Satan get in the way of truth. In the words of Hamlet as he spoke to Horatio, both of whom had

---

1. Marshall W. Fishwick, *Faust Revisited, Some Thoughts on Satan* (New York: The Seabury Press: 1963), 4.

just seen a ghost, "There are more things in heaven and earth, Horatio, than are dreamt of in your philosophy."

One of the most interesting texts in the entire Bible is found in 1 Samuel 28. King Saul, who had outlawed all mediums, decided that he needed to see one. In desperation he visited a witch in Endor. Although the witch was a charlatan, people really believed she talked to the spirits of the dead, and she laughed all the way to the bank.

Saul went to her and said, "Call up Samuel!" Samuel was the dead prophet of God, and the old woman, having gone through her routine often, began to get out her bag of tricks. And then, to her horror, Samuel actually appeared. Now, dear reader, that is enough to shake the false teeth out of a mound of Poli-Grip. The text reads, "When the woman saw Samuel, she cried out with a loud voice" (1 Sam. 28:12). You would have too. It was rather traumatic to have all her presuppositions shattered so quickly, to be confronted with a reality she couldn't explain. Time after time, I have seen Christians absolutely devastated because they disregarded the clear teaching of the Bible on the person of Satan. When they had an encounter with him, they were not prepared to deal with his reality.

That brings me to the other thing I want to say to you about Satan: Information from Scripture that you find difficult to accept ought to be filed away or put on the back burner for a while. The time will come when that information will be of great value. Nothing is included in Scripture that wasn't meant to be there, and all of it, including the doctrine of Satan, was given that we might "be adequate [mature], equipped for every good work." (2 Tim. 3:17)

Did you hear about the corn farmer who decided to become a chicken farmer? He went to the feed store and ordered a hundred baby chicks. A week passed and he went back to the same feed store and ordered another hundred. The owner of the feed store said, "Why in the world do you need another hundred? What happened?" The farmer said, "The first hundred died, and I can't figure out why. I'm either planting them too deep or watering them too much." The farmer had tried to transfer his knowledge of corn farming over to chicken farming, and it just didn't work.

Christians who try to deal with the supernatural world by using natural laws have the same problem. One of the interesting things about Jesus is the way He reverses so much of what we think is true. He says that we are to love our enemies and pray for those who persecute us. He says that if we want to lead we have to serve, and that if we want to find our lives we have to lose them. And He says that we are blessed when we are poor in heart, and meek, and in mourning. He is saying to His followers, "You are now going to be living on a different plane, a supernatural one, and the rules are different." That's how we should approach the teaching of the Bible on the subject of Satan. It may seem silly and outdated, but use it anyway. You might be surprised.

I have been walking with Jesus many years now, and while I'm still a sinner and have not reached the level of maturity I ought to have reached, I find the Bible's teaching on the supernatural in general, and on Satan in particular, more and more helpful. I used to laugh at demons—until I ran into a demon-possessed man and it scared me to death. I used to say that all healing was psychosomatic, until my little girl was made well because people prayed. I used to think that the devil was the "metaphorical personification of evil"—until I heard him laughing.

Satan's Work at the Cross

The Cross was more than just a good man dying. On the Cross Jesus encountered and defeated all the forces of evil. If you had been standing on Calvary that day, and if you could have had your spiritual blindness removed, you would have seen a cosmic battle taking place. And you would have seen Jesus Christ win the battle. Jesus was referring to the Cross when He told His disciples, "Now judgment is upon this world; now the ruler of this world shall be cast out" (John 12:31). The writer of Hebrews said, "Since then the children share flesh and blood, He Himself likewise also partook of the same, that through death He might render powerless him who had the power of death, that is, the devil" (Heb. 2:14). I used to wonder why Jesus had to die. Wouldn't it have been better if He had lived a long, full life? Wouldn't it have been better if He had stayed on earth longer and taught us more? Thirty-three years was simply not enough. When I became a Christian, I understood the necessity of Christ's death for my salvation. And with increasing maturity in Christ, I have seen more of the nature of Satan and of Christ's victory over him on the Cross. Let me share with you what I have learned.

Evil's Hatred of Good

For one thing, I have learned it was inevitable that Jesus die on the Cross, because evil cannot endure the presence of good. Scripture speaks of how Jesus "endured such hostility by sinners against Himself" (Heb. 12:3). There was something about the goodness of Christ that made it inevitable that evil would try to destroy it.

In Calvin Miller's *The Singer*, there is a very moving description of the Singer's death. The Singer, you may remember, was the allegorical figure of Jesus; Hater was Satan, and Earthmaker was God. The Singer was being tortured on a great torture machine, and as he died Hater cried out:

"You give me joy and music you will never hear, Singer. Groan for me. Scream the fire that fills your soul. Spew the venom of your grudge upon the city. Never have I known the triumph of my hate till now."

He rose and walked across the beam and stepped upon a cable. The added strain drew the manacles into the wrists of the dying Singer.

"Check-mate, Singer!" He howled into the mist and the shrieking of his laughter absorbed into the opaque air.

The Singer felt the agony of dying, the mutilated pain of a hundred thousand men all dying at one time.

With an agility of delight the Hater danced his way around the armature and struggled on the ropes. He looked into the fog again and shouted, "Your move, Earthmaker."

"I have you crying, Earthmaker. You can never glory in your universal riches, for I have made you poor. And there is none to pity you . . .

"You started crying when they broke his hands. Can it be that the agony which plunges you in grief can wash my soul with joy?"[2]

One of the central themes of great literature is the necessary destruction of either evil by good or good by evil. That is one of the themes you will find being played out in William Faulkner's stories about Yoknapatawpha County, and in the plays of Tennessee Williams. In C. S. Lewis's *Perelandra*, and in the other two books of his space trilogy, the character named Weston is the personification of evil. When he was not trying to plunge Perelandra into a darkness similar to the darkness of earth, he was destroying beauty. He took magnificently beautiful flowers and crushed them, and he loved to kill small animals with his long fingernails.

A woman once told me that she hated her sister, and in an outburst of anger she cried, "I wish she were dead!" In the silence that followed I asked her why. Speaking through her sobs, she said, "Because she is beautiful and good." Ugliness always seeks the destruction of beauty, and evil seeks the destruction of good.

Anti-Semitism started when the Holy Torah made the Jews different and good. The world doesn't like different and good

---

2. Calvin Miller, *The Singer*, 123–25.

people, and thus the evil of the world was bent on their destruction. Their righteousness flowing from the law of God was an open invitation to persecution. They were different, and the world's ideal is bland evil. It is a law of human nature: Evil tries to destroy good.

And so we begin to see something of the necessity of the Cross. The absolute goodness and purity of Jesus Christ was an absolute threat to the absolute evil and hatred of Satan. Almost two thousand years have come and gone since Calvary, and things haven't changed much. Evil still tries to destroy good; purity is still the world's proper subject for jokes; honesty is held in derision; and love is washed out in a philosophy of doing your own thing. Just as Satan was behind the Cross, so he is behind the destruction of good in our time. When messiahs hang on crosses, and when good men and women do bad, Satan laughs and laughs and laughs.

Evil's Hatred of Truth

There is more instruction to garner from the Cross on Calvary. Jesus had to die because a lie cannot stand in the face of truth. In John 1:9–10 we read, "There was the true light which, coming into the world, enlightens every man. He was in the world, and the world was made through Him, and the world did not know Him." Later John wrote, "For the law was given through Moses; grace and truth were realized through Jesus Christ" (1:17). And as the hour of His death approached, Jesus said to those who were plotting His death,

> You are seeking to kill Me, a man who has told you the truth, which I heard from God; this Abraham did not do. You are doing the deeds of your father. . . . You are of your father the devil, and you want to do the desires of your father. He was a murderer from the beginning, and does not stand in the truth, because there is no truth in him. Whenever he speaks a lie,

he speaks from his own nature; for he is a liar, and the father
of lies. (John 8:40–41, 44)

I was on a radio talk show when a woman called in and, as if
speaking from Sinai, said something I knew to be an outright lie.
I questioned her on it, and do you know what she did? She
yelled very loudly and accused me of calling her a liar. When
people are caught in lies, they usually grow very angry and
defensive. If you have ever been caught in a lie, you know the
experience. When that woman became angry at being caught in
a lie, she was manifesting one of the operative principles of the
universe: A liar unmasked as a liar will hedge, will become
angry, and finally will grow destructive. Jesus said, "I am the
way, and the truth" (John 14:6), and in that statement we begin
to see why He had to die.

One of my daughters brought home a Confederate bill. As
we examined it, I was reminded of the time when Jefferson
Davis fled from Richmond with three wagons loaded with Confederate money. Davis and the money were captured by Union
soldiers, and the Confederate bills were piled up, bale upon
bale, in the camp of the Union soldiers. It was cold and windy,
and the soldiers were bored and hungry. They decided to play
poker with the Confederate money, and they played for a hundred thousand dollars a game. But do you know something?
The next morning the soldiers were just as hungry and tired and
cold as they had been the night before.

That is the way it is with the world—one great hustle for
worthless tender. And Jesus came to tell us so. He said, "Look,
you're missing the whole reason you were born. That stuff is
worthless." He said, "Do not lay up for yourselves treasures
upon earth, where moth and rust destroy, and where thieves
break in and steal. But lay up for yourselves treasures in heaven,
where neither moth nor rust destroys, and where thieves do not
break in or steal; for where your treasure is, there will your heart
be also." (Matt. 6:19–21)

And Satan looked up from his poker game, took the stogie out of his mouth, focused his eyes on the One who had interrupted the game, pulled out a gun, and shot Him. The Law: A lie will always try to destroy truth. That law still operates, and that is why the men and women of God who bear the truth are persecuted.

It is dangerous, you know, to utter God's truth in the world. His truth says that in order to recognize His sovereignty you must give up your own. You either accept His sovereignty or you kill it. Truth was crucified on Calvary; truth was placed in the tomb; and when that dead Man got up and walked, truth was set loose on the world where no Cross would ever stop it again. Jesus had to die because a lie will always seek to destroy the truth, and Satan is the father of lies.

Evil's Hatred of Life

There is one more "law" we can learn from the death of Christ on the Cross: Death will always try to consume and destroy life. Jesus said, "You are of your father the devil, and you want to do the desires of your father. He was a murderer from the beginning" (John 8:44). When Jesus died on the Cross, Satan, the "murderer," was filled with joy. Peter gave this advice: "Be on the alert. Your adversary, the devil, prowls about like a roaring lion, seeking someone to devour." (1 Peter 5:8)

Scientists tell us there may be "black holes" in space. As I understand it, a black hole results when the hydrogen fuel of a star burns out and, as the star's core stops burning, gravity pulls the shell inward and crushes all the atoms. I understand that a handful of material from a black hole could weigh several thousand tons. At any rate, the black hole draws everything into it, including light. Thus, you can't see it in space.

Satan is like that. Everything that is light is sucked into his sphere to become dark and black. He delights in death, destruction, and darkness. The Cross was simply Satan's effort to do what comes naturally. There the battle between good and evil reached its climax.

Satan is real, and he is out to get you. That's the bad news.

The Good News of Jesus' Victory

Now let's look at some good news. If you have read the above and have concluded that the biblical faith is dualistic (composed of two equal and opposing forces, one good and one evil), you have made a terrible mistake. Nothing could be farther from the truth.

The Bible teaches that there *are* two forces, one good and one evil; however, it does not teach that the two forces are equal. The Bible teaches that God is sovereign over everything and that Satan's existence is only tolerated because he fits into God's plan. In the book of Job, there is an interesting dialogue between God and Satan:

> There was a day when the sons of God came to present themselves before the LORD, and Satan also came among them. And the LORD said to Satan, "From where do you come?" Then Satan answered the LORD and said, "From roaming about on the earth and walking around on it." And the LORD said to Satan, "Have you considered My servant Job? For there is no one like him on the earth, a blameless and upright man, fearing God and turning away from evil." Then Satan answered the LORD, "Does Job fear God for nothing? Hast Thou not made a hedge about him and his house and all that he has, on every side? Thou hast blessed the work of his hands, and his possessions have increased in the land. But put forth Thy hand now and touch all that he has; he will surely curse Thee to Thy face." Then the LORD said to Satan, "Behold, all that he has is in your power, only do not put forth

your hand on him." So Satan departed from the presence of
the LORD. (Job 1:6–12)

There are several interesting things about that passage, but
the most important is that Satan had to ask God's permission
before going after Job. Satan is God's lackey, acting only with
His permission.

Not only is Satan far less than God's equal; Satan will one
day actually glorify God along with the rest of creation. The
Scripture says, "Therefore also God highly exalted Him [Christ],
and bestowed on Him the name which is above every name, that
at the name of Jesus every knee should bow, of those who are in
heaven, and on earth, and under the earth, and that every
tongue should confess that Jesus Christ is Lord, to the glory of
God the Father" (Phil. 2:9–11). The Christian faith is not dualistic. Everything was created for one purpose, to glorify God.
And even Satan will one day glorify God.

That is part of the good news, but there is more: The Christian is playing in a ball game that has been fixed. The contest
has already been decided. The victory has already been won.
Satan will come out on the short end of the stick. You can count
on it because on the Cross of Christ Satan's end was secured,
and in the empty tomb the believer's victory was made manifest.
The Scripture says,

Since the children have flesh and blood, he too shared in their
humanity so that by his death he might destroy him who
holds the power of death—that is, the devil—and free those
who all their lives were held in slavery by their fear of death.
(Heb. 2:14–15, NIV)

The fact of Satan's defeat, however, should not lull the Christian into believing that he is powerless. Martin Luther told his
followers they ought to be very careful of Satan because he had
years of experience on them. If the battle is to be won, it must

be won by Christ in our lives, not by our power to resist and fight. As the writer of Hebrews goes on to say, "He is able to help those who are being tempted." (verse 18)

Dealing With Satan

Very quickly, let me give you some practical helps for dealing with Satan. God has given us the gift of prayer in the name of Christ, and that gift ought to be utilized. When Jesus taught His disciples to pray, He told them to pray to be delivered from "the evil one." (See Matt. 6:13. The familiar King James Version reads, "deliver us from evil"; but the Greek actually implies a personal "evil one," and most modern translations render it that way.) And when Jesus was warning Peter, He said, "Simon, Simon, behold, Satan has demanded permission to sift you like wheat; but I have prayed for you, that your faith may not fail; and you, when once you have turned again, strengthen your brothers" (Luke 22:31–32). When you are overwhelmed by temptation, burdened with the evil within your own heart and from others, depressed beyond the help of modern pop psychology, try praying in the name of Christ that Satan be banished. It is a powerful prayer.

The second tool God has given the Christian to appropriate the victory already won is faith. Faith is a part of our Christian armor, described in the sixth chapter of Ephesians: "In addition to all, taking up the shield of faith with which you will be able to extinguish all the flaming missiles of the evil one" (Eph. 6:16). Another word for faith is *trust*. Paul was saying that the Christian ought to be developing a walk with Christ that enables him to trust Christ's ability to deal with Satan. In the movie *My Bodyguard*, a boy was being intimidated by the bullies at his high school. He talked one big, mean kid into being his bodyguard, and thereafter he was able to stand up to all the intimidation. You have a Bodyguard, and only a fool will wander far from Him.

Third, the Christian can appropriate Christ's victory over

Satan with watchfulness. Peter said, "Be of sober spirit, be on the alert. Your adversary, the devil, prowls about like a roaring lion" (1 Peter 5:8). Don't assume you are too spiritual to be attacked by the tempter; nobody is. Don't think that because you have read your Bible and prayed you are free from the possibility of evil; nobody is. Don't think there is some magic formula that will exempt you from the devil's plans; there isn't. The closer you draw to Jesus, the closer Satan will try to draw to you. If you know that, you will be watchful. After almost every spiritual victory in your life you will be open to depression, doubt, pride, anger, and evil thoughts. Someone has said, "If you didn't meet Satan this morning, it's a pretty good indication you were going in the same direction." To be forewarned is to be forearmed!

Fourth, in order to appropriate the victory over Satan won for you on the Cross, be feisty in your resistance. The Bible says, "But resist him [Satan], firm in your faith" (1 Peter 5:9). James said, "Resist the devil and he will flee from you" (James 4:7). It's dangerous to believe that if you do nothing, everything will be okay. God didn't design the world that way, and He didn't design you that way. You were meant to be active in your walk with Christ.

Now, please notice that I didn't tell you to fight the battle yourself, or insist that your own heroic effort will defeat Satan. That isn't what the Scriptures mean when they talk about resistance. The passage I quoted from James has two parts: "Submit therefore to God," *then*, "Resist the devil and he will flee from you." If you do that, Satan will know that you belong to Christ and that you stand with His hedge about you . . . so he will flee.

Do you remember in *The Wizard of Oz* when Dorothy, the lion, the tin man, and the scarecrow finally reached the Wizard? The Wizard was an awe-inspiring figure frightening everyone except, of course, Toto, Dorothy's little dog. Toto ran to the curtain and pulled it back, revealing a little man pulling the levers that controlled the gigantic, fake wizard. Satan is sort of like that wizard. If you confront him in the power of Christ, if you resist him, you will find that he isn't as big as you thought. There's an old English proverb that says, "Fear knocked at the door, faith answered, and no one was there." Apply that proverb to Satan and it fits: Satan knocked at the door, faith answered, and no one was there.

Truth is a strong weapon against Satan. Paul says, "Stand firm therefore, having girded your loins with truth." And again, "Take the helmet of salvation, and the sword of the Spirit, which is the word of God" (Eph. 6:14, 17). The best way to deal with the "father of lies" is to apply a heavy dose of truth. Satan will tell you that you are powerless against him; he will say you don't belong to Christ; he will make you afraid and tell you the Bible isn't true. When that happens, speak the truth: "When He [God] had disarmed the rulers and authorities [Satan and his demonic helpers], He made a public display of them, having triumphed over them through Him [Christ]" (Col. 2:15). That is a fact, and you can stand on it.

I once visited a small church in the Philippines, nestled back in the mountains. As we made the long journey to the church, I really didn't expect to find very many people or a very exciting ministry. When we drove up to the church, however, it was difficult to get past the large crowd of people standing in the streets trying to get in.

After the service I asked the young pastor about the great and excited crowd. He told me that two weeks before there had been a woman in their village who through involvement with the occult had become possessed by a demon. Everything had been tried to help her. The local witch doctor had been called, and he had spent days trying to deal with the satanic power. The woman's family was frantic and had no one else to turn to but the pastor and his elders. He told me they had gone in the power of Christ and had rebuked Satan and prayed for the woman. The people of the village had started coming to the church in droves because they had seen the power of God.

I asked him what happened when he went to see the woman. I will never forget his answer: "Jesus won. Satan lost."

For Personal Insight or Group Discussion

1. How do you see the power of Satan manifest in the world around you? In your own life? Do you feel that you tend to focus too little or too much on Satan's power?

2. Why do those who do good and tell the truth so often suffer because of it? (Compare John 8:40–41 with John 14:6.)

3. What truth did Jesus proclaim in Matthew 6:19-21? What lie does the devil constantly tell us instead of this truth?

4. How does Christ's resurrection help us overcome the power of Satan in our lives? (See Heb. 2:14-15, 1 Tim. 1:10.)

5. "The closer you draw to Jesus, the closer Satan will try to draw to you." Have you found that to be true in your own life?

6. How well have you been able to "resist" the devil? (1 Pet. 5:9, James 4:7.) What steps might you take to "build up your resistance?"

Four

If Jesus has come...
Love Has Won

If Jesus has come . . .
Love Has Won

I am convinced that neither death, nor life, nor angels, nor principalities, nor things present, nor things to come, nor powers, nor height, nor depth, nor any other created thing, shall be able to separate us from the love of God, which is in Christ Jesus our Lord. (Romans 8:38–39)

There is an old story about a man who dreamed he was given a tour of heaven and hell. In hell he saw a very long table that stretched for miles. On the table were platters of the most delicious food he had ever seen. Thousands upon thousands of people, as far as he could see, were sitting on both sides of the table. When he examined the scene more closely, he noticed that the people sitting at the table were not getting much to eat, because they were required to eat with four-foot-long spoons. You can imagine how difficult that would be; you would be able to get the food on the spoon, but to get it into your mouth would be difficult if not impossible. The man noticed the people in hell were angry at one another, withdrawn, and bitter. And most of all, he noticed, they were hungry!

Much to his astonishment, the man saw the same scene in heaven: the long table, the delicious food, and the four-foot-long spoons. But in heaven the people were happy and well-fed. And right away he saw the reason for that big difference between heaven and hell: In heaven, the people were feeding each other across the table!

That is a good story, and it certainly has a lot of truth in it, but does it really tell the whole truth? Could it be that it is just a nice story and doesn't reflect the way the world really works? Will people ever love each other and work together that well, even in heaven? In the last chapter we saw that hate tries to destroy love. In his superb book *Reflections of a Neoconservative*, Irving Kristol titled an essay, "Machiavelli and the Profanation of Politics." In his essay, he delineated the harsh and "practical" views of Machiavellianism in regard to power politics divorced from any moral system. At the close of the essay Kristol wrote,

> There have been three major figures in the history of Western thought during the last five centuries who have rejected Christianity, not for its failure to live up to its values, but because they repudiated these values themselves. The three are Machiavelli, de Sade, and Nietzsche. A great part of the intellectual history of the modern era can be told in terms of the efforts of a civilization still Christian, to come to terms with Machiavelli in politics, de Sade in sex, Nietzsche in philosophy. These efforts have been ingenious, but hardly successful. The "save morality"of Christianity is constantly in retreat before the revolt of "the masters" with every new modus vivendi an unstable armistice. Heidegger has even gone so far as to say that the struggle is over—that with Nietzsche the Christian epoch draws to a close.[1]

Paul said there are three things that will last forever, faith, hope, and love, and that the greatest of the three is love (see 1 Cor. 13:13). But is that really true? Do you ever wonder if

---

1. Irving Kristol, *Reflections of a Neoconservative* (New York: Basic Books, 1983), 134–35.

perhaps Christians have chosen the losing side? Do you ever look around, see the prosperity and success of those who have divorced themselves from love, and wonder if maybe *they* are right? Is love really better than hate?

Those are fair questions, and the Bible is not afraid to pose them honestly:

> For I was envious of the arrogant,
> As I saw the prosperity of the wicked.
> For there are no pains in their death;
> And their body is fat.
> They are not in trouble as other men;
> Nor are they plagued like mankind.
> Therefore pride is their necklace;
> The garment of violence covers them.
> Their eye bulges from fatness;
> The imaginations of their heart run riot.
> They mock, and wickedly speak of oppression;
> They speak from on high.
> They have set their mouth against the heavens,
> And their tongue parades through the earth. (Ps. 73:3–9)

> And they say, "How does God know?
> And is there knowledge with the Most High?"
> Behold, these are the wicked;
> And always at ease, they have increased in wealth.
> Surely in vain I have kept my heart pure,
> And washed my hands in innocence;
> For I have been stricken all day long,
> And chastened every morning. (verses 11–14)

Is love really stronger than hate? When the last page of history has been turned, will the hero be Jesus or Hitler? If we have enemies, is it better to love them or to hate them? We live in a dog-eat-dog world: Should we really even consider the way of love? Isn't love the way of weakness? Those are the questions posed by this chapter. The Bible's answer is clear: God is love, and God rules the universe. Because He is love and is sovereign, the final outcome of love will be victory. The Bible says that the best way to deal with people is to love them—even our enemies. We are promised that in the end love will destroy hate. That all sounds good, but we weren't sure it was true until Jesus came. Because Jesus has come, love has conquered—because *He* has conquered.

Jesus, the Proof of Love's Conquest

Jesus is God's key to *knowing* that love is stronger than hate. Let me illustrate: Perhaps you remember when the University of Miami won the national football championship. Those of us who live in Miami will never forget it. For years the UM football team had received very little attention. When we finally had the best football team in the nation, nobody could believe it. But we knew they were the best. We knew that Howard Schnellenberger was the best football coach in the nation and that nobody was going to beat the University of Miami.

Of course our "knowing" could have been attributed to wishful thinking, partisan football fever, or hometown hopes. But when Miami received its invitation to the Orange Bowl against the football giants of Nebraska, we had a chance to check out our knowing. And when the University of Miami emerged victorious, our knowing was affirmed by everyone else in the nation. Before that Orange Bowl, UM was the best in the nation. The Orange Bowl did not change the reality; it just confirmed it. Miami didn't win at the Orange Bowl and thus *become* the best; they won at the Orange Bowl because they *were* the best.

For years, those who knew God had known that He was love and that His ultimate victory was assured. But in Christ their knowing was affirmed. The reality of love's victory was made clear. That is what John meant when he wrote concerning love, "Beloved, I am not writing a new commandment to you, but an old commandment which you have had from the beginning; the old commandment is the word which you have heard. On the other hand, I am writing a new commandment to you, which is true in Him and in you, because the darkness is passing away, and the true light is already shining" (1 John 2:7–8).

A little later in that letter John wrote, "Beloved, let us love one another, for love is from God; and everyone who loves is born of God and knows God. The one who does not love does not know God, for God is love" (4:7–8). That sounds good, but how do we know it's true? "By this the love of God was manifested in us, that God has sent His only begotten Son into the world so that we might live through Him." (verse 9)

The story of Christmas is a love story. Don't be confused by the trinkets and the glitter. It's not even about babies, stables, and wise men. Christmas is about love. "For God so loved the world, that He gave His only begotten Son" (John 3:16). Love came down at Christmas.

The Vocabulary of Love

As God relates to us, He uses our vocabulary. He communicates with us through the words and ideas of our human experience. Consider, for instance, the sacrament of the Lord's Supper. It was no accident that Jesus used common, everyday things like bread and wine. In the twenty-third psalm, God related to His people with green pastures, still waters, and death. He spoke to us in our own terms. That is why Calvin called the Bible "God's baby talk." When you think about God and all His power and greatness, the fact that He relates to us at all is amazing; but the fact that He relates with a language we can understand is absolutely astounding.

That's one reason God says so much about his love for us. Love is universal. Do you remember the first time you fell in love? Of course it was puppy love, but it was real to the puppy. Your only interest had been cowboys and Indians and mud pies until you discovered that special boy or girl.

In our congregation there is a young man who decided on a unique way to propose to his beloved. His name is Steve Vensel, and Steve never does anything in a bland way. He had some friends invite his sweetheart, Dory, to a picnic in a public park. What she didn't know was that he had dressed as a knight in shining armor, had rented a horse, and was waiting in the trees off to the side of the park. When Dory was settled down for the picnic, he approached her on his horse, climbed down, and knelt before her. This is what he said: "Fair Princess, I have searched for thee. I have journeyed far and long in my quest, and many sorrows have I known. Yet in vain has not my quest been, for who doth cause my heart to sing but the King Himself. And my heart sings for thee. I am but a knight in the service of the Prince. Riches of gold and silver and jewels I cannot give. But that which is most precious have I guarded for this day. My heart, my love, my very life have I reserved for thee. These are the gifts I offer. . . . Alas, Princess, it is thee I love. It is with thee I wish to endeavor life's journey. Wouldst thou take my hand in marriage? Wouldst thou ride with me and me alone?" Needless to say, Dory accepted his proposal.

When we talk about love, we can all understand it to one degree or another because we have all been in love. And it is no accident that the relationship between God and His creation is also one of love. Listen to some of the Scriptures relating to the way God loves: "Indeed, He loves the people; all Thy holy ones are in Thy hand, and they followed in Thy steps" (Deut. 33:3). "Just as a father has compassion on his children, so the LORD has compassion on those who fear Him" (Ps. 103:13). "I have loved you with an everlasting love" (Jer. 31:3). God relates to us in the language of love, a language we can understand.

In order to understand the kind of love about which the Scripture speaks, it is important that we stop for a moment and define it. We live in a culture that mimics the real love manifested in the Bible: "What the world needs now is love, sweet love." "Lay a little love on me, baby." As has been pointed out so often, the Greeks had a number of different words that we translate into our English word *love*. One of their words meant to love someone sexually, another to love someone as a brother, another to like someone, and still another to like some*thing*. But the best Greek word, and the one used to describe God's love, was the word *agape*. *Agape* love is that kind of determined love that wills and does the best for someone regardless of his or her response.

Some things can be defined in terms of what they are, but others can be defined only in terms of what they do. Love is of the latter. Love, in order to be love, must express itself. The Bible says that God is love; and if that is true, His love must find a tangible expression. That is what the incarnation is all about.

God's "Problems" in Loving Us

Have you ever considered the fact that God has a problem with His love for us? We can identify with His problem because we all have had the experience of trying to relate to someone who didn't even know he or she was being loved. As God tries to love us, He is faced with a number of questions. The first question is this: What do you do if you love someone and the person you love doesn't even know you exist? Of course, you can try to get that person to notice you. I can remember the first time I was in love. I had no idea in the world how to meet this special girl until I saw her in a drugstore standing near the soda fountain. I decided it was my one chance; so I bought two milk shakes and took one to her. But she didn't want a milk shake. Furthermore, she thought I was an arrogant stranger trying to bring her one without even asking. She turned and walked away, leaving me standing there with two milk shakes in my hands. I decided I didn't want a milk shake, either. You must be very careful when you want to love someone who doesn't even know you exist.

Perhaps the best way to get the person you love to notice you is to get someone to introduce you. I am often asked by a young man or woman to make an introduction to someone he or she has seen across the church. (One of my great joys is to make an introduction, see the couple grow together, get married, and produce little Presbyterians!)

The prophets were God's "introducers." The God of the universe, the God of Abraham, Isaac, and Jacob, was doing no more and no less than sending messages through them to a people He loved. *Eternity in Their Hearts* is a fascinating book by Don Richardson that shows how cultures have been prepared for hearing the gospel. In every culture, in every place, God has planted the seeds of His love by revealing Himself in various ways. For example, I grew up in the mountains of North Carolina near the Cherokee Indian reservation. Recently, on a visit home, my wife and I attended a lecture on Cherokee theology, and we were astounded. The Indians of North Carolina had a theological system so sophisticated that it is difficult to understand where they got it. Before the missionaries ever came to the Cherokee, they believed there was one God and that He manifested Himself in three Persons. They believed idolatry was wrong and that the God they worshiped was a loving God. I believe God was preparing a culture for the manifestation of His love.

It is an old movie plot, and it has been used over and over again. The woman is either a minor actress in a play or a dancer in a musical. She has a secret admirer in the audience every night. Night after night, she receives a dozen roses with no name attached, just a card that reads, "From a secret admirer." She begins to wonder who he could be; she dreams of what he will look like; she thinks of him often. And then finally he asks her to dinner, and they fall in love and live happily ever after.

That is what God has done. We didn't know Him, but He knew us and loved us. He sent roses; sometimes the roses were the prophets, at other times the gentle push of a cultural idea. Sometimes He whispered His love in the trees and the sunsets.

And then, at Christmas, God signed the card.

I read the other day of a clergyman who counsels engaged couples. He said that when he asks a couple how long they have known each other, almost without exception the woman will say three or four years and the man will say two or three years. He drew the following conclusions: The man didn't even know the woman existed for a whole year. She knew him and loved him even before he knew she existed. Likewise, God knew us and loved us even before we knew He existed. John said, "In this is love, not that we loved God, but that He loved us and sent His Son to be the propitiation for our sins. . . . We love, because He first loved us." (1 John 4:10, 19)

God faces a second question regarding His love for us: What do you do if you love someone and the person you love doesn't love you back? Unrequited love is a horrible thing, and the interesting thing about it is that the people who suffer from it almost always do the wrong thing. They manipulate: "I have cancer, and I only have a short time to live. Couldn't you find it in your heart to give me a little time?" They use force: "I know you don't love me, but if you don't learn to, I'll beat up your little brother." They use persistence: "You have no choice. I am going to pressure you and pursue you until you give up." They use guilt: "I have loved you for so long; I have taken you places; I have stood with you and defended you. The least you could do is love me a little. If you don't, I'll kill myself and you'll be sorry."

I heard about a young woman in Sicily who was not interested in the affections of her persistent suitor. After trying to discourage him as much as possible, she finally called the police and had a restraining order issued against him. He was prevented from seeing or calling her on penalty of going to jail. Of course the restraining order was not enough to discourage him, and he was finally thrown in jail. But every time he got out of jail, he went to the nearest phone and called the woman. The last I heard, he had been in jail eleven times. When someone doesn't love you, it can be a horrible thing.

God is wise in the ways of love. He knows that if you want someone to love you back, you have to be gentle. You catch a loved one the same way you catch a mountain trout. You do it very carefully and very gently. That, dear reader, is what God did at Christmas. He knew that love takes a while. He knew us. And so He whispered. That is why He came as a baby instead of as a king.

I have a German shepherd named Calvin. He came to us one night almost by accident. Someone had beaten him and intimidated him, and when Calvin wouldn't respond, he was set loose. He showed up at our house at three in the morning. When Calvin first came to us, he was afraid of men, probably because he had been beaten by a man. He related quite well to my daughters and my wife, but not to me. I tried everything to get him to come to me. I tried feeding him, petting him, and talking softly to him, but nothing seemed to work. After a few months, however, he seemed to begin deciding I wasn't going to hurt him. Some evenings I would be reading the paper and would feel a soft nudge at my elbow. I would turn around to see Calvin running in the opposite direction. I gave it time, and little by little Calvin and I have become friends. In order to get Calvin to return my love, I had to be very gentle and patient.

To a much greater degree, God expressed His love in a gentle and patient way. "And this will be a sign for you: you will find a baby wrapped in cloths, and lying in a manger." (Luke 2:12)

A third question is this: What do you do if you love someone who is not worthy of your love? A young man told me that he had given up dating. I asked him if he was shy, and he said that wasn't his problem. He said, "The problem is that I can't find a woman who will please Mother." His mother had decided that no woman was good enough for her son.

The Father God decided that, too. The only difference between God and that young man's mother is that she was wrong in her opinion . . . and God hit the nail on the head.

One of the problems with "celebrity Christianity" is that people begin to get the idea that God only loves those who are attractive: If you are beautiful, charming, or athletic, then God will love you. Let me tell you something: There are no attractive people, as far as God's holiness is concerned. When you measure beauty, charm, and athletic prowess by perfection, there is no such thing as beauty, charm, or athletic prowess. How much truer is this if you measure human goodness by perfection? You have to cry out with the prophet, "The heart is more deceitful than all else and is desperately sick; who can understand it?" (Jer. 17:9)

A few summers ago, both of my daughters were in other countries on mission projects. My older daughter, Robin, was in Europe witnessing in youth hostels in a number of countries, and Jennifer was in the Dominican Republic helping build churches. Needless to say, I was terribly worried about them both. I knew how I *ought* to have felt. I ought to have been proud that they were sharing their faith in Christ. And I suppose I did feel such pride. I ought to have been glad that my daughters loved God enough to go to a sinful world, and I guess I really was. But mostly I worried, and sometimes I thought, "There isn't a sinner in the world who is worth either of my daughters." Those were the thoughts I had one particular day, and I was telling the Father about them. But then He reminded me that if He had felt that way, I would never have known His love. He reminded me again that He loved the world, that He gave His only Son, and that nobody in the world was worthy of that gift.

I read the other day of a teenager who bought his girlfriend an orchid. It was the first orchid he had ever bought and the first one she had ever received. There was a card with the orchid, and it read, "With all my love, and most of my allowance." Well, God said, "With all of my love, and all of my allowance. I love you this much."

What do you do when the one you love is not worthy of your love? You don't stop loving, because worth is not a factor in love. Hosea learned that when he was commanded by God to marry the prostitute Gomer. God said to Hosea that that was what love was all about. You don't explain love; who knows why a princess loves an ugly frog? She just does. God loved us when we didn't deserve it, and that is what the incarnation is all about.

Finally, what do you do if you love someone who is never going to love you back? You've heard the saying, "When you love something, set it free, and if it never returns to you, it was never meant to be." There is something insipid about that, but there is some truth to it, too. Love that is forced is not love. It is manipulation.

I can force my family to show the signs of love, but I can't force them to love me—even though I am bigger and stronger than they are. I can say to my daughters, "You love me or I will never speak to you again." I can say to them, "I will hit you and hurt you if you don't love me." Then they may hug me and kiss me and do nice things for me, but they will never love me. Do you know why? Because love, in order to be love, must have a choice.

The incarnation was the time when the God of the universe served the ball into the world's court. He said: "I love you. I have demonstrated My love, but I will not force it on you. You must come to Me yourself. You don't have to come with a gift, or with purity, or with a love like Mine. But you must come. If you are thirsty I will give you living water, because I love you. But you must drink. If you are hungry I will give you the bread of life, because I love you. But you must eat. If you are tired and weary I will give you rest, because I love you. But you must lean on Me. If you are sinful and dirty I will forgive you and clean you up, because I love you. But you must come."

This is the dark side of the incarnation. If Jesus has come, love has conquered hate: But there are those who will never know love's victory, because they have placed themselves on the wrong side of the battlefield.

The Absolutes of Love

As we end this chapter, let's look at the four absolutes of love. First, God is love (see 1 John 4:8). God doesn't just love; He doesn't just act in a loving way; He doesn't just do loving things. He *is* love. And if God is love, then everything that flows from His being is loving. The world is a manifestation of His love; all creation points to the power of His love. The hymnist Frederick Faber put it very well:

> For the love of God is broader
> Than the measure of man's mind,
> And the heart of the Eternal
> Is most wonderfully kind.

You don't have to plead with the sun to shine, nor do you have to hope that water is wet. It is stupid to pray that fire will burn or that an apple will have seeds. The wetness of water, the shining of the sun, the burning of fire, and the seeds of apples are all the attributes of those things. Just so, love is an attribute of God. He is love.

The second absolute is this: Jesus is the perfect manifestation of God's love. Jesus said, "Just as the Father has loved Me, I have also loved you; abide in My love" (John 15:9). Commenting on the incarnation, John said, "The Father loves the Son, and has given all things into His hand" (John 3:35). And in his first letter, John said, "By this the love of God was manifested in us, that God has sent His only begotten Son into the world so that we might live through Him." (1 John 4:9)

It was World War II, and the battle was fierce. Jerry had been wounded and was dying in a no man's land. Jerry's buddy pleaded with his sergeant to be able to go to his friend's aid. At first the sergeant refused. He said, "Are you crazy? You'll be killed, too. There isn't anything you or anyone else can do." But Jim persisted, and finally the sergeant relented and allowed him to go. Jim made his way under the barbed wire and through the mud and slush. Two hours later he came back carrying the body of his dead friend. The sergeant said, "See, I told you it wasn't worth it. He's dead."

"No sir," replied the soldier, "it was worth it. When I got to him he was still alive, and he said, 'Jim, I knew you would come.'"

That is real love, because love will always act. Jesus is the loving action of God. The difference between Jim's trip into no man's land and Jesus' trip into no man's land is not in the love. The love was the same. The difference between Jim and Jesus is that Jesus brought us back alive.

The third absolute is that the Holy Spirit creates the same love in us that is an attribute of God and is manifested in Jesus. "The love of God has been poured out within our hearts through the Holy Spirit who was given to us." (Romans 5:5)

You can't manufacture love. The raw materials are simply not available. They are only sold in one place, and that is the store owned and operated by the Holy Spirit. To those who have turned to Christ and His manifestation of love on the Cross, the Holy Spirit gives a gift far more important than teaching, prophecy, tongues, knowledge, healing, wisdom, or faith. The Holy Spirit gives God's people love.

Love is not natural to human beings. It has been said that you have to be taught to hate. That's a lie. You don't have to be taught to hate. Hate comes naturally. Watch children at play and take particular note of their essential cruelty toward one another. Watch adults at play, and you will see the same cruelty, only hidden better. Racism, war, and selfishness are reflections of normal humanity. Thomas Brown's little ditty is a true picture of the human experience:

> I do not love thee, Dr. Fell;
> The reason why I cannot tell;
> But this I know, and know full well:
> I do not love thee, Dr. Fell.

My dear friend Ara Tchividjian lost his father during the Armenian genocide in Turkey. As soon as his own oldest son, Stephan, was old enough to understand, he gave him a gun and said, "Son, if you ever meet the people who killed your grandfather, you will kill them. If you do not kill them, you are no longer my son."

Some years later Ara Tchividjian became a Christian. On the day he encountered the love of Christ, he went to Stephan and asked for the gun. He told his son, "If I ever meet those who killed your grandfather, I will throw my arms around them and tell them that I love them." Where did he get that kind of love? I'll tell you. He got it from the Spirit of God, the God who is love and who has manifested that love in His Son. There is one final absolute: Not only is the first person of the Trinity, God the Father, love; not only is the second person of the Trinity, God the Son, the manifestation of love; not only is the third person of the Trinity, God the Holy Spirit, the creator of love; but the church, the focal point of the Trinity's love, is effective and powerful because of love. In the great hymn of love in 1 Corinthians 13, Paul said,

> If I speak with the tongues of men and of angels, but do not have love, I have become a noisy gong or a clanging cymbal. And if I have the gift of prophecy, and know all mysteries and all knowledge; and if I have all faith, so as to remove mountains, but do not have love, I am nothing. And if I give all my possessions to feed the poor, and if I deliver my body to be burned, but do not have love, it profits me nothing. . . . But

now abide faith, hope, love, these three; but the greatest of
these is love. (1 Cor. 13:1–3, 13)

What is God saying? It is an astounding revelation. He is
saying, "I don't care who you are, what you do, how much you
have, how great your gifts are, or how much you know; if you
don't have love, you are a clanging cymbal, useless for anything
except making noise."

When all is said and done, hate will be destroyed. You see,
hate can only exist in opposition to love. It is not something
that exists in its own right. Love, white-hot love, will burn up
everything that is not love. The road of hate is the road of ultimate destruction. How do I know? Because a dead man got up
and walked, and when He got out of the grave, the love of the
Father that He manifested was let loose on the world, where it
will never be destroyed—ever.

The apostle John was perhaps the greatest teacher about the
love of Jesus. Running throughout both the Gospel of John and
his three letters is the theme of love. Tradition says that when
the Roman proconsul in Ephesus commanded John to deny
Christ, he replied, "It behooves us to obey God more than man.
Hence I will neither deny Christ nor desist from preaching His
name, but will continue the course of my ministry which I
received from the Lord."[2] At this reply the proconsul tortured
John and finally exiled him to the island of Patmos.

If ever there was a man who had reason to hate, harbor bit-
terness, or be angry, it was the apostle John. It is said, however,
that he never lost the love Christ had given him. He returned to
his beloved Ephesus during the last days of his life, and on the
day of his death he was carried by his friends on a pallet to the
church assembly where he had served so long and faithfully as
pastor. The congregation asked him to speak to them one more
time. He made one comment: "Love one another."

---

2. Emil G. Kraeling, *The Disciples* (Chicago: Rand McNally & Company, 1966), 149.

The people in the congregation asked John why he always said this, and he replied: "Because there is nothing else!"[3]

That's it. If Jesus has come, love really has conquered.

---

3. H. S. Vigeveno, *Thirteen Men Who Changed the World* (Glendale: Regal Books, 1967), 126.

For Personal Insight or Group Discussion

1. How would you define love? How would most of your friends define it? What common mistakes do we make in trying to understand what love is all about?

2. How can we know the correct definition of love? (1 John 2:7–9.)

3. How was the incarnation of God the Son in the person of Jesus Christ an expression of God the Father's love for the world? (John 3:16)

4. Do you agree that love is best defined in terms of what it does? How well do your actions or the actions of people you know help define love? (Rom. 5:5.)

5. What has been your experience in learning to love "problem people"? What has that experience taught you about God's "problems" in loving us?

6. Thinking of both the good and the evil in our world today, how confidently can you say that "love has won"?

Five

If Jesus has come . . .
Death Has Died

If Jesus has come . . . Death Has Died

Christ Jesus . . . abolished death, and brought life and immortality to light through the gospel. (2 Timothy 1:10)

One of the most fascinating occurrences of our time is the scientific interest generated by the Shroud of Turin. Many believe it is the Shroud in which the corpse of Jesus was wrapped before His resurrection. The Shroud's history is complex, and many details are obscure. Its existence was not generally known until 1357, when it was exhibited in the French provincial town of Lirey.

In 1898, Secondo Pia was allowed to photograph the Shroud for the first time. To his astonishment, when he looked at the negatives of his pictures, he found they presented a highly detailed picture of a man who had been crucified.

The next showing of the Shroud took place in 1931, when detailed photographs were taken by Giuseppe Enrie. The photographs he took that year became the basis of study by physicians and scientists in France, England, Italy, Germany, and the United States. Their conclusions were not unanimous in every detail, but they all agreed on one matter: The imprints in the Shroud are those of a human corpse in a pronounced state of rigor mortis.

In 1978, there was a major development in the study of the Shroud. A team of scientists, known as the Shroud of Turin Research Project, converged on Turin, Italy. The Catholic church had allowed an object of faith to be inspected with the neutral analytical tools of modern science, and it was an opportunity not to be missed. Dozens of scientists of every religious belief and unbelief were invited to examine the Shroud to settle once and for all its authenticity. It was the most thorough examination of a religious relic by the scientific community in history. Millions of dollars in sophisticated testing equipment was taken to the Renaissance reception room in the royal palace of the House of Savoy. For five days, the most rigorous and detailed testing of the Shroud took place. Then the results were tested and retested in the laboratories of scientists in Europe and the United States. The preliminary conclusions from that study were nothing less than astounding.

First, they concluded that the Shroud and the image on it are not counterfeit. The Shroud contained a corpse of a crucified man about five feet ten inches tall. The facial expression is peaceful, especially compared to the tortured and punctured body.

Second, the anatomy pictured on the Shroud shows details that weren't even known until the eighteenth century. An artist would have had to travel six hundred years into the future to learn the information necessary to produce a counterfeit.

Third, there are actual blood stains on the fourteen-foot Shroud. There is also an amazing accuracy in terms of blood flow and consistency. The corpse in the Shroud died with nails through the upper part of his hands, and a nail was driven through his feet. The blood stains show there was a crown of thorns or a similar object on his forehead. There was a lance wound in his side.

Fourth, pollen discovered in the threads of the Shroud has been shown to be from first-century Palestine.

Fifth, there has been a computer enhancement of the image on the Shroud that makes the image three-dimensional. That image is especially interesting, because it shows that coins were placed over the eyes of the corpse. The coins bear an amazing resemblance to those issued by Pontius Pilate in the years A.D. 31–34.

Sixth, the back of the Shroud shows small lash marks. The details of these wounds are amazing in that they show exactly the marks that would have been left by a Roman flagrum, an instrument of torture used much like a whip.

I could go on and on.[1]

By far the most interesting mystery about the Shroud of Turin is how the corpse got out of the Shroud. The facts militate against the body's being removed from the Shroud by any human means, because the blood stains have not been smudged. Further, the body in the Shroud did not decompose while wrapped in it. Pathologists are sure the man was dead, but the scientific tests found no evidence of decomposition beyond the initial signs of death. That, of course, indicates the body was in the Shroud for a very short time.

The scientific tests suggest the image on the Shroud was caused by a very intense and momentary blast of heat and light, much like radiation. It has been impossible for scientists to duplicate the image. Dr. Bucklin, the deputy medical examiner for Los Angeles County said, "The medical data from the Shroud supports the resurrection. When this medical information is combined with the physical, chemical, and historical facts, there is strong evidence for Jesus' resurrection." The medical facts have convinced Dr. Bucklin that the Shroud of Turin is the burial cloth of Jesus Christ.[2]

Did the Shroud of Turin contain the body of Jesus? Maybe. However, the reaction of many to the scientific data surrounding the Shroud is more fascinating than the data itself. Rarely has

---

1. Those readers who would like more details about the Shroud of Turin should read *Verdict on the Shroud*, by Kenneth Stevenson and Gary Habermas (Wayne, Penn: Banbury Books, 1981) and an earlier book by Ian Wilson titled *The Shroud of Turin* (Garden City, N.Y.: Doubleday and Company, 1979).
2. Stevenson and Habermas, *Verdict*, 206.

opposition to a scientific investigation been so shrill. When the facts began to indicate that Jesus was the body in the Shroud, and when there was indication of a miraculous removal of the body, the forces began to line up on the other side. That was nothing new. In 1902, Yves Delage, an agnostic professor of comparative anatomy at the Sorbonne, became convinced that the corpse in the Shroud was none other than the historic Jesus. When Delage made his findings known to the French Academy of Sciences, many of his colleagues were outraged that he would even discuss the subject, and the Academy refused to publish his work. Delage was understandably surprised and hurt. More recently, numerous articles and editorials, including one in the *New York Times*, have been critical of the authenticity of the Shroud and the validity of the Shroud of Turin Research Project.

One magazine, *National Review*, did a generally favorable article on the Shroud, and the response they received from their readers was immediate and harsh. In his "Notes and Asides" column, William F. Buckley answered:

> As for us, we fail to understand the manifest hostility toward the Shroud on the part of some Christians. Would they be equally interested or ostensibly uninterested in a possible or problem portrait of Xerxes? of Alexander the Great? Is it possible that the details of the Shroud are just too "literal" for an enlightened liberal sensibility? Is it somehow bad manners to suggest that Christian claims about what happened to Jesus are, in fact, true?[3]

Subsequent to this book's first publication, the skeptics apparently won the day when, in the early fall of 1988, a team of scientists used carbon-14 testing to determine once and for all the age of the Shroud. When these tests suggested that the Shroud was a medieval forgery, the doubters were ecstatic, and

---

3. Stevenson and Habermas, *Verdict*, 233.

articles about the Shroud swiftly disappeared from the secular media—and, for the most part, from the religious media as well. This sudden fading of public interest notwithstanding, a significant number of the scientists who have devoted their lives to studying the Shroud remain convinced of its authenticity, and believe that there were serious flaws in the way the carbon-14 testing was conducted.[4]

The Nature of Unbelief

You need to understand I'm not suggesting that faith in the resurrection of Christ is dependent on the authenticity of the Shroud of Turin. Instead, I wanted to underline the fact that most people don't believe in the resurrection, and if they were confronted with absolute, factual verification of the event, they still would not believe in it. Most people don't have trouble believing in a "spiritual" resurrection, or believing that the resurrection is a myth that teaches truth; but to believe that a dead man actually got out of the grave is another thing altogether. C. S. Lewis once said he knew only one person who claimed to have seen a ghost, and she didn't believe in immortality.

Here is the point: If the resurrection of Christ is not an absolute, space-time fact, then the whole Christian faith is silly. Paul put it this way: "If Christ has not been raised, your faith is worthless; you are still in your sins" (1 Cor. 15:17). Make no mistake about it, the resurrection of Christ is important, because the whole superstructure of the Christian faith is built on the assertion that Jesus didn't stay dead. If in fact He didn't stay dead, the implications are fantastic. If, on the other hand, He *did* stay dead, you need to get as much of what this world offers as you possibly can in the time you have left, because there will be nothing else.

---

4. The authors of *Verdict on the Shroud* have recently updated their research in response to the significant developments since that book's 1981 publication. See Kenneth Stevenson and Gary Habermas, *The Shroud and the Controversy* (Nashville: Thomas Nelson Publishers, 1990).

Unbelief That Denies Facts

Unbelief fascinates me, especially unbelief that denies facts to the detriment of the unbeliever. You would think the news that a man rose from the dead and said that we could, too, would be seen as good news. You would think the news of the resurrection would be greeted with laughter and joy. But, incredibly, some people stand on the sidelines and throw rocks and shout, "I don't believe it, I won't believe it, and there is nothing you can say to me that will cause me to believe it."

The religious establishment at the time of Christ's death and resurrection displayed this kind of unbelief. In Matthew 27:62–65, there is a curious reaction to even the possibility of the resurrection. It takes place the day after Jesus was crucified:

> Now on the next day, which is the one after the preparation, the chief priests and the Pharisees gathered together with Pilate, and said, "Sir, we remember that when He was still alive that deceiver said, 'After three days I am to rise again.' Therefore, give orders for the grave to be made secure until the third day, lest the disciples come and steal Him away and say to the people, 'He has risen from the dead,' and the last deception will be worse than the first." Pilate said to them, "You have a guard; go, make it as secure as you know how." And they went and made the grave secure, and along with the guard they set a seal on the stone.

That night, an angel came to the tomb and "rolled away the stone and sat upon it" (Matt. 28:2). The soldiers posted to watch the tomb "shook for fear of him, and became like dead men" (verse 4). When they regained consciousness, Jesus was gone. A few verses later, Matthew records what happened when those soldiers reported the event to the chief priests:

> Some of the guard came into the city and reported to the chief

priests all that had happened. And when they had assembled with the elders and counseled together, they gave a large sum of money to the soldiers, and said, "You are to say, 'His disciples came by night and stole Him away while we were asleep.'" (Matt. 28:11–13)

A part of the ministry God has given me is a ministry to skeptics. Having been one for so long myself, I determined that if I ever found some honest answers to my honest questions, I was going to share them with others who had honest questions. But the problem with the chief priests was that they didn't have any questions. They had the answers, and nothing was going to change their minds. I don't know the reason; perhaps it was a vested interest; maybe it was a fear of being wrong. But whatever the reason, the kind of unbelief the priests manifested was *unexamined* unbelief. After dealing with skeptics for a number of years and after being one for just as many years, I have found that a closed, skeptical mind is one of the great wonders of the world. Somehow we have accepted the idea that fanaticism is the particular malady of the religious. That simply is not true. You haven't seen anything until you have met a closed-minded skeptic. At least a closed-minded Christian has some hope and meaning. A closed-minded skeptic has to fight to remain miserable. The chief priests sealed the tomb without the possibility (much less the hope) that a dead man was going to get out of the tomb on His own power. And when they heard from those who were there that the dead man had actually arisen, they still refused to believe. If they had examined the soldiers' story, they would have been confronted with a surprise of monumental proportions. But you see, closed-minded people never check the facts.

Unbelief That Is Uncertain

There is another kind of unbelief, however, that is dear to the heart of God. We have seen that sort of unbelief in the apostle Thomas. After Jesus had been placed in the tomb, Thomas, like the others, was broken. Everything had come apart, and the devastation in his life was beyond calculation. Then one evening Jesus appeared to the disciples. Mind you, Jesus was no ghost that evening. He was the real Jesus, who could eat a meal and teach a lesson. As you can imagine, it was an exciting revelation, but Thomas wasn't with the disciples at the time.

John recounted the incident: "The other disciples therefore were saying to him, 'We have seen the Lord!' But he said to them, 'Unless I shall see in His hands the imprint of the nails, and put my finger into the place of the nails, and put my hand into His side, I will not believe.'" (John 20:25)

For eight days Thomas boiled in the juices of his own doubt. I can imagine that those eight days were horrible. The questions must have haunted him: *What if Jesus did come back from the dead? Can I afford to invest in any more hope? Where will I go to find some answers?* I suspect that each time Thomas got to the point of hope, he closed his eyes and heard the hammer driving the nails through Jesus' hands and thought to himself, I *just can't go through the loss again.*

The next time Jesus appeared to the disciples, however, Thomas was with them:

> Jesus came, the doors having been shut, and stood in their midst, and said, "Peace be with you." Then He said to Thomas, "Reach here your finger, and see My hands; and reach here your hand, and put it into My side; and be not unbelieving, but believing." Thomas answered and said to Him, "My Lord and my God!" Jesus said to him, "Because you have seen Me, have you believed? Blessed are they who did not see, and yet believed." (John 20:26–29)

We sometimes have a "Skeptics Forum" at our church. It is a group of unbelievers who meet to see if the Christian faith is true. I am the only Christian among them, and the skeptics set the agenda. The sessions go for about ten weeks, and each session deals with one question, such as, Does God exist? Is the Bible true? How do you explain suffering if you have a compassionate God? I usually speak to the question for about ten minutes, and then for the next two hours the skeptics go after me. I could fill the rest of this book with incidents that have happened in Skeptics Forum, but one of the most moving incidents happened the evening a young woman began to cry. She was a teacher who had given up the Christian faith as a teenager. I asked her the reason for her tears, and she said, "Oh, God, I wish this stuff were true." Thomas was like that, and God met his questions with answers that absolutely took his breath away.

Unbelief That Is Unaware

There is another kind of unbelief we ought to consider before leaving the subject. It is the unbelief that is unaware. In Luke 24, you will remember, there were two travelers on the road to a village called Emmaus, which was seven miles from Jerusalem. The crucifixion of Jesus had taken place three days before, and they were discussing the rumor of Jesus' resurrection. We'll let Luke tell the story:

> And it came about that while they were conversing and discussing, Jesus Himself approached, and began traveling with them. But their eyes were prevented from recognizing Him. And He said to them, "What are these words that you are exchanging with one another as you are walking?" And they stood still, looking sad. And one of them, named Cleopas, answered and said to Him, "Are you the only one visiting Jerusalem and unaware of the things which have happened here in these days?" (Luke 24:15–18)

The two men then explained to Jesus all that had happened, including the reports from those who had seen Jesus after He had risen from the dead. Luke continues:

> And He said to them, "O foolish men and slow of heart to believe in all that the prophets have spoken! Was it not necessary for the Christ to suffer these things and to enter into His glory?" And beginning with Moses and with all the prophets, He explained to them the things concerning Himself in all the Scriptures. And they approached the village where they were going, and He acted as though He would go farther. And they urged Him, saying, "Stay with us, for it is getting toward evening, and the day is now nearly over." And He went in to stay with them. And it came about that when He had reclined at table with them, He took the bread and blessed it, and breaking it, He began giving it to them. And their eyes were opened and they recognized Him; and He vanished from their sight. And they said to one another, "Were not our hearts burning within us while He was speaking to us on the road, while He was explaining the Scriptures to us?" (Luke 24:25–32)

My friend Tom Haggai, who was a friend of the famous Baptist pastor Robert G. Lee, told me one time why Lee was such a great evangelist. Early in his ministry, Dr. Lee was awakened one evening by a phone call telling him about a young woman in her twenties who had taken an overdose of drugs. The caller told Dr. Lee she was in the hospital and was dying. He asked Dr. Lee if he would come.

Dr. Lee went to visit the woman. He came close to her bed, bent over her dying body, and said, "My dear, I'm Pastor Lee, and I have come to talk to you."

"Oh, Dr. Lee," she said, "I have heard you preach many times."

"I'm glad," he replied, "but I have come to talk to you about Christ. I would like you to receive Christ as your Savior."

"Dr. Lee," she said, "I have heard you preach many times."

"My dear," he persisted, "you are close to death, and it is of eternal importance that you receive Christ."

"Dr. Lee," she again said, "I have heard you preach many times."

He determined that if anyone heard him preach again, they would remember what they needed to know about Christ.

The dying woman and the two travelers on the road to Emmaus are examples of unbelief based on a lack of knowledge. It is unbelief that is unaware.

And thus, in regard to the resurrection of Christ, we have three kinds of unbelief: unbelief that is unexamined; unbelief that is uncertain; and unbelief that is unaware. The first kind of unbelief must simply be ignored. For some reason, we Christians seem to think we ought to give ourselves to those who would rather be left alone. But if time is limited (and it is), if there are those who have already made up their minds despite the facts (and there are), and if there are people who really want to know the truth (and there are), then we ought to waste as little time as possible on those whose unbelief is deliberate.

However, it is terribly important that all unbelievers hear the truth. If you are an unbeliever, let me give you some facts.

Facts About the Resurrection

Fact Number One: The disciples of Jesus of Nazareth were changed because something happened that absolutely "blew their minds." They claimed they had seen Jesus—after He died. It is possible, I suppose, to deny that they saw Jesus after His death, but it is impossible to say they didn't see *something*. Too much changed to deny that.

If you will, go with me to the upper room where the disciples gathered after the death of Christ. There never was a more depressed group of men. Everything for which they had worked and prayed had come to an abrupt end on the town garbage heap between two thieves. The dreams of a lifetime were in dust at their feet. Jesus was dead. Peter said, "I am going fishing" (John 21:3). That's all there was left to do. Matthew would return to his tax tables, James and John to their fishing business, and Nathanael to his dreaming. They would remember the days when Christ had lived among them; they would remember and be sad for what might have been. They would go back to their old lives as sadder but wiser men.

They were afraid, too. Suppose you had been a follower of Jesus and had watched Him die. It would probably have dawned on you that the executioners didn't like you a whole lot more than they liked Him. You would think, *It could happen to me, too.* There are no good ways to die, but if you had a choice, crucifixion would not be it. And so these disciples gathered in the upper room—because when you're afraid it's better to be afraid with someone else.

Now think of these men only a few days later, on the day of Pentecost. Were these the same men who had huddled together in that upper room? They looked the same; they had the same accents, the same names—but they weren't the same. Peter, for instance, the coward who had denied Christ three times, stood before a crowd of thousands and spoke in a booming, assured voice:

> Men of Judea, and all you who live in Jerusalem, let this be known to you, and give heed to my words. . . . Men of Israel, listen to these words: Jesus the Nazarene, a man attested to you by God with miracles and wonders and signs which God performed through Him in your midst, just as you yourselves know—this Man, delivered up by the predetermined plan and foreknowledge of God, you nailed to a cross by the hands of godless men and put Him to death. And God raised Him up again, putting an end to the agony of death, since it was impossible for Him to be held in its power. (Acts 2:14, 22–24)

That, I would submit, was not the same Peter who wouldn't take a stand before the crucifixion.

The question then is this: What caused the change?

And consider what they *didn't* say after they had changed: They didn't say, "We have some nice things to say about a martyr who was a great teacher." No, they didn't proclaim a new, wonderful teaching about love. They didn't talk about religion. They said they had seen a dead man walking! They said they had eaten with Him, talked to Him, and touched Him. That is a fact that requires explanation.

Fact Number Two: The disciples were *willing to die* for their claim that they had seen Jesus after His death. Of the original disciples, only John died of old age, and as we have seen even he suffered torture and exile for his faith. Tradition says James was run through with a sword, and Peter was crucified upside-down because he said he was not worthy to die as his Master had died.

Now let me ask you a question: Would you insist on telling a lie, over and over again, if you knew it took you one step closer to death every time you told it? Would you participate in a conspiracy designed to bring about your own death, and a horrible death at that? Would you willingly drive nails into your own coffin? Of course you wouldn't! Jesus' disciples wouldn't have, either. Yet they were willing to die for their claim that Jesus had risen. That is a fact that needs an explanation.

Fact Number Three: The disciples were not the only ones who saw Jesus after His death. There were more than five hundred people (see 1 Cor. 15:6) who saw Him. If one person told us he had seen a man getting out of a grave, we would call the men in white jackets. If two people told us a dead man had gotten up and walked, we would reply, "You've got to be kidding!" If ten people told us they had just come from a graveyard where a dead man had risen from a grave, we probably wouldn't believe them, but at least we would go down to the graveyard and check. But if five hundred people told us the same story, we would have to give serious consideration to their testimonies.

I once served as pastor in a little village on Cape Cod. One of the members of the church was the parks commissioner for the village. There wasn't much for a parks commissioner to do except mow the graveyard and keep the hedges trimmed. On one occasion, this man was cleaning off a headstone over a grave that was more than a hundred years old. A hundred years ago, no one required grave liners, so the old graves had a tendency to cave in. On this occasion the grave gave way, and he fell into the hole. He told me later that as he was climbing out of the hole, someone drove through the cemetery and saw him. The driver evidently thought my friend was a dead man coming out of a grave, because he couldn't drive out of that graveyard fast enough!

What if that man had come to the church and told us what he had seen? We would have kidded him and then explained what had really happened. But if five hundred people see a dead man walking and they tell you not only that they saw Him alive after they had seen Him die, but also that they talked to Him . . . that is a fact that needs some explanation.

Fact Number Four: The religious and governmental institutions had a vested interest in stopping the rapid spread of the Christian faith, but they could not do it. By the fourth century Christians had conquered the Roman Empire. The Christian faith had swept away the government that had tried to persecute it out of existence. Now, let me ask you a question: Why wasn't Rome able to stop the spread of Christianity? It should have been a relatively simple matter. With just a little detective work, the leaders could have discovered what Jesus' disciples had done with His corpse, and they could have brought it forth for everyone to see. But they didn't do that. And let me tell you why they didn't: There was no corpse! The dead body had gotten up and walked away! The leaders who most wanted to destroy the Christian faith couldn't do it. That is a fact that needs an explanation.

Fact Number Five: The first-century witnesses to the resurrection of Jesus must have been credible witnesses, or their testimonies would not have held up. We live in a provincial age: We believe that every age but ours was superstitious and credulous. We think we are the only generation that ever had doubts. That's silly, of course, and we ought to remember that first-century people had just as many doubts as we have about corpses getting out of graves. However, they had an advantage over us. They were able to talk to the witnesses. They could cross-examine them, check out their facts, and make sure their stories held water. If their testimonies hadn't held up, the Christian faith would have died in the first century. It didn't. That is a fact that needs an explanation.

Fact Number Six: The church of Christ covered the Western world by the fourth century. There were simply no rivals. Do you seriously believe that a religious movement built on a lie could accomplish that? It is said that when Augustine was informed about the fall of Rome, he was saddened. But he said, "I am the citizen of a city that shall never fall." Out of the ruins of Rome, Augustine fashioned his monumental work, *City of God.* How do you explain the phenomenal growth of the Christian church? It is a fact that needs explanation.

Of course these are only a few of the facts surrounding the resurrection of Jesus Christ. I would suggest the interested reader pursue the matter further. Frank Morrison's *Who Moved the Stone?* and Josh McDowell's *Evidence That Demands a Verdict, Vol. 1,* can be obtained at any Christian bookstore and are good popular works on the subject.

The Importance of the Resurrection

Perhaps you are saying, "So what?" If Jesus did get up out of the grave (and He did), what difference does it make? It makes a lot of difference. It means that everything He said is true, that the teaching He gave is practical, that the life He lived and still lives can make your life different.

Let's talk about the difference Christ's resurrection makes in terms of the fact that we're all going to die, and the fact that we're all are afraid of death.

Death is an awesome reality, one with which most of us would rather not deal. We do everything possible to cover it up, to hide its reality. Our culture has become expert in the art of making a corpse look alive. How often have you heard someone standing at an open coffin say, "My, Sam (or Sally, or Joe) really looks good." He doesn't look good! He's dead! We cover the corpse with polished wood, heap it with flowers, dim the lighting, and place it in a beautiful setting. We do everything possible to hide the reality that someone has become a corpse.

How much better it was when the family had to do all the "dirty work" of preparing the loved one for burial. The family made the coffin, laid out the corpse, used their home for the wake, dug the hole, and buried the loved one. That may seem harsh, but psychologically it was very healthy. People faced the reality of death and were able to deal with it. Grief was hard work, but it was short. Today years sometimes pass before a family fully recovers from a loss. And still we don't want to think about death. And when we do, we usually say something silly like, "Death is a normal part of living," or, "Just like birth, death is natural." Let me tell you something important: Death is not normal. You were not created to die. In fact, the Bible teaches that you were created to live forever. When Jesus died on the Cross and rose from the dead, He did it so that you could fulfill your eternal destiny of living forever. Paul made a startling statement in his first letter to the Corinthians:

Now I say this, brethren, that flesh and blood cannot inherit the kingdom of God; nor does the perishable inherit the imperishable. Behold, I tell you a mystery; we shall not all sleep [i.e., die], but we shall all be changed, in a moment, in the twinkling of an eye, at the last trumpet; for the trumpet will sound, and the dead will be raised imperishable, and we shall be changed. For this perishable must put on the imperishable, and this mortal must put on immortality. But when this perishable will have put on the imperishable, and this mortal will have put on immortality, then will come about the saying that is written, "Death is swallowed up in victory. O death, where is your victory? O death, where is your sting?" The sting of death is sin, and the power of sin is the law; but thanks be to God, who gives us the victory through our Lord Jesus Christ. Therefore, my beloved brethren, be steadfast, immovable, always abounding in the work of the Lord, knowing that your toil is not in vain in the Lord. (1 Cor. 15:50–58)

Do you know why you have to die? You have to die because you have sinned. The Bible says that the wages of sin is death (see Rom. 6:23). No one wants to hear that; nevertheless, it is true. If you jump off a fifteen-story building, you are going to kill yourself. If you put your hand on a hot stove, you are going to get burned. If you sin, you are going to die. On the Cross, Jesus took our sin and declared us forgiven. The penalty of sin (death) has been borne by Christ for us. Because the sin is gone, the death is gone. And Jesus came back from the grave to prove it.

Jesus said, "Because I live, you shall live also" (John 14:19). If Jesus stayed in the grave, the first part of His statement is not true; and therefore, it follows logically that the second part of His statement is not true either. If Jesus did not live, then we won't. But if He did live, if He did get up out of the grave, if He did break the bonds of death, then *we will too.* He promised that we would; and He is the only one who has the right to make that promise.

The next time you face the reality of death, don't cover it up; fight it with the truth: Death has died. It died at the hands of Jesus our Lord. Jesus has risen from the dead, and has given immortality to all who follow Him. That is a fact, and you can hang your hat on it.

For Personal Insight or Group Discussion

1. Why is the Christian faith "worthless" (1 Cor. 15:17) if Jesus did not rise from the dead?

2. This chapter describes three types of people who do not believe in the resurrection. If you are not a believer, do you see yourself fitting into any of these categories? If you are a believer, how would you explain your faith to each of these three kinds of nonbelievers?

3. Take some time to review carefully the following six "Facts About the Resurrection." Do these facts convince you that Jesus did, in fact, rise from the dead?

> *Fact 1:* The disciples of Jesus of Nazareth were dramatically changed, because of something that happened after Jesus died.

> *Fact 2:* The disciples were *willing to die* for their claim that they had seen Jesus after His death.

> *Fact 3:* Altogether, more than five hundred people saw Jesus alive after His death.

> *Fact 4:* The religious and governmental institutions had a vested interest in stopping the rapid spread of the Christian faith, but they could not do it.

> *Fact 5:* The first-century witnesses to the resurrection must have been credible witnesses, because otherwise their testimonies would not have held up.

> *Fact 6:* Following the death of Jesus, the church He founded spread quickly throughout the Western

world—an amazing accomplishment if in fact He remained dead.

4. If you are convinced that Jesus rose from the dead, what difference does it make it you in this life? After you die? (1 Cor. 15:50–58)

Six

If Jesus has come . . .
I'm Forgiven

If Jesus has come ...
I'm Forgiven

In Him we have redemption through His blood, the forgiveness of our trespasses, according to the riches of His grace, which He lavished upon us. (Ephesians 1:7–8)

A few years ago while speaking at a conference I told about how I had been a pastor before knowing God. After the session a man came up to me with an obvious question. "Steve," he asked, "if you didn't know God, why, in God's name, did you go into the ministry?" I didn't have an answer for him that evening, but I've thought about the question a lot since then.

There are several reasons why someone who doesn't know God goes into the ministry. For instance, someone can enter the ministry because he or she would *like* to know God. Religious friends told me I had a glib tongue and would be a good preacher. I was interested in philosophy, and there wasn't much of a market for philosophers. I had a vague desire to help people, and preference tests showed I was high in the particular proclivities that would make me a good pastor. But, to be perfectly honest with you, the main reason I entered the ministry was to allay guilt.

A lot of that guilt was unnecessary. It was a psychological, undefined, unproductive guilt. Nevertheless, it hurt just as much as the real thing. Real guilt is based on a real violation of God's standard, and real guilt needs real repentance. When the repentance takes place there is a sense of relief and freedom. "For the sorrow that is according to the will of God produces a repentance without regret, leading to salvation; but the sorrow of the world produces death" (2 Cor. 7:10). I had real, definable guilt, too, and felt justifiably guilty about many things.

My guilt caused me to turn to a profession where I could be a "good" person and perhaps feel better about myself. Now, I'm sure that I have been called to be a pastor. I'm doing what God told me to do, and if He used guilt to motivate me to do His will, I'm glad. He didn't check with me first. But motivation by guilt presents some serious problems, not the least being that guilty people make others feel guilty. And in case you haven't noticed, the best way to get people to do church work is to make them feel guilty. It's always easy to get people involved in evangelism, visiting, stewardship, or anything else by making them feel guilty. Of course, their motivation doesn't last very long, but it certainly gets them started. As I read back over the sermons of those early days, I blush to see that I had become a master of motivating people with guilt.

Then I noticed an amazing change in the content of my sermons. Somewhere in the early years of my ministry, I stopped trying to make people feel guilty. I know the reason for the change: I discovered that God is a great forgiver. I learned what it really means to be forgiven. I understood what Christ did for me on the Cross. I didn't feel guilty anymore, and therefore didn't have to make others feel guilty. I didn't have to manipulate people anymore. I didn't have to assuage my guilt by getting others to share it. I was free.

Please understand me. There is legitimate guilt. A lot of folks who don't feel guilty ought to. When Christians (or unbelievers, for that matter) violate God's law, they ought to feel guilty. We still need to talk about sin. But if truth is taught, the

Holy Spirit will do the convicting (see John 16:8), not us. When the Holy Spirit convicts people, He always does it for the right reasons.

In Matthew 5:17–18 Jesus said, "Do not think that I came to abolish the Law or the Prophets; I did not come to abolish, but to fulfill. For truly I say to you, until heaven and earth pass away, not the smallest letter or stroke shall pass away from the Law, until all is accomplished." Did Jesus change the law? Of course not. If you want to know what God wants you to do, all you have to do is check the law. When Jews say that the law, the Holy Torah, is the greatest gift God ever gave, they are right. It is a tremendous thing to know what God wants from His creatures. If, for instance, I don't know what my boss wants me to do in my job, I'm going to have some serious problems. I'll always have an overwhelming sense of anxiety about whether or not I'm doing the job I have been hired to do. So, accurate information about how I am to do my job is important. And if that's true about my job, it's much more true about how I'm to live my life.

God's law reflects His information not only on the right way to live, but also on the best way to live. The law tells us where life's minefields are. It tells us the best way to live in order to have reasonably balanced and happy lives.

This raises an obvious question: If all that is true about the law of God, and if Jesus didn't come to change the law, what did He do about the law? Listen! He came to give us two important gifts, power and forgiveness—power to obey the law, and forgiveness when we don't. Wouldn't it be nice to have the power to be different from what you are right now? Wouldn't you like to have power over sin? These questions are an advertisement for the next chapter, where we will talk about the amazing example Jesus has given to His own.

Necessary Bad News

For the rest of this chapter I want to talk to you about the second of those gifts, forgiveness. But you can't talk about forgiveness unless you talk about why there is a need for forgiveness. That means you can't hear the good news until you hear the bad news. The bad news is that, believe it or not, you are not a good person. Remember the verse we read from Jeremiah? "The heart is more deceitful than all else and is desperately sick; who can understand it?" (Jer. 17:9). The Bible also says, "We have already charged that both Jews and Greeks are all under sin; as it is written, 'There is none righteous, not even one; there is none who understands, there is none who seeks for God; all have turned aside, together they have become useless; there is none who does good, there is not even one'" (Rom. 3:9–12). And what if we claim to be an exception to that all-encompassing indictment? "If we say that we have no sin, we are deceiving ourselves, and the truth is not in us" (1 John 1:8). What the Bible says about us isn't very nice; nevertheless, it is true.

My friend Fred Smith says that there are two basic anthropological views, two views of man that determine everything we think and do in education, government, and the church. The first view is that man is basically good with a proclivity for evil, and the second is that man is basically bad with a proclivity for good. If you believe the first of the two propositions, you may believe in democracy, for instance, because people are good and can be trusted. If you believe in the second proposition, you may believe in democracy because people aren't good and no one person is good enough to have too much power.

In *The Federalist*, Alexander Hamilton defended the idea of a union as opposed to separate states living in close harmony with one another:

A man must be far gone in Utopian speculations who can seriously doubt that, if these States should either be wholly disunited, or only united impartial confederacies, the subdivisions into which they might be thrown would have frequent and violent contests with each other. To presume a want of motives for such contests as an argument against their existence, would be to forget that men are ambitious, vindictive, and rapacious. To look for a continuation of harmony between a number of independent, unconnected sovereignties in the same neighbourhood, would be to disregard the uniform course of human events, and to set at defiance the accumulated experience of ages.[1]

One of the interesting things about liberal Christianity is that it believes idealistically in the perfectibility of human nature. The reason liberal Christianity is dying is that an institution built on a lie eventually dies. When all the restraints of society, religion, and culture are removed, human nature is not very pretty. I love C. S. Lewis's designation of earth as "the silent planet" in his science fiction. If you haven't read the *Space Trilogy*, you should. Lewis suggested that all the other planets of the universe are without redemption because they didn't need to be redeemed. One planet, the earth, is fallen and dark. It is the silent planet.

That is an accurate description of earth. In all of human history, earth has enjoyed only a few years of relative peace. It has been a planet rife with selfishness, strife, ambition, and war; a planet where *holocaust* is not a word for one historical incident but for many: Cambodia, Turkey, Germany, to name a few. There is something warped about our planet and its people, and any philosophical, political, social, or religious system that fails to take that into account is doomed to failure.

Author William Golding clearly shows us the degeneracy of human nature. In *Lord of the Flies*, a group of boys is stranded

---

1. Alexander Hamilton, James Madison, John Jay, *The Federalist,* Great Books of the Western World, Robert Hutchins, ed. (Chicago: Encyclopaedia Britannica, 1952), 39.

on a deserted island and civilized behavior deteriorates into chaos, destruction, and murder. It is an accurate assessment of the way things really are.

Let's get a little more personal. There was a time in my life when I believed there were two kinds of people in the world: good people and bad people. The good people went to church on Sunday, were honest in their dealings with others, didn't cheat on their wives or husbands, and didn't smoke or drink too much. The bad people were those who had turned away from God, were dishonest in their dealings with others, cheated on their wives or husbands, and smoked and drank too much. I wasn't a pastor long before discovering I was right that there are two kinds of people in the world, but wrong about who they are. Actually, there are bad people who know they're bad, and bad people who *don't* know they're bad. You fall into one or the other of those categories.

The Big Ten

Perhaps the best way to determine whether we're sinners is to review the "Big Ten," the Ten Commandments. People are always saying to me that they have made a few mistakes but that they certainly are not *bad*. I have found it helpful to get out my Bible, turn to Exodus 20, and go over the requirements of God.

The first commandment God gave the world was not to have any other gods before Him (see Ex. 20:3). "Well," you say, "I certainly haven't violated that commandment. I have been brought up in the church worshiping the true God; I had godly parents who taught me the truth about the true God; I never have been involved in any religious movement where any other god was worshiped." But think for a moment: Have you ever placed your job, your family, or your desires above God?

The Westminster Larger Catechism says this about the first commandment:

The duties required in the first commandment are: the knowing and acknowledging of God to be the only true God, and our God [okay so far]; and to worship and glorify Him accordingly [still okay]; by thinking, meditating, remembering, highly esteeming, honoring, adoring, choosing, loving, desiring, fearing of Him; believing Him; trusting, hoping, delighting, rejoicing in Him [how are you doing?]; being zealous for Him; calling upon Him, giving all praise and thanks, and yielding all obedience and submission to Him with the whole man; being careful in all things to please Him, and sorrowful when in anything He is offended; and walking humbly with Him.

You say you have some trouble with all of that? Guilty!

In His second commandment, God told us we should not make any graven images and worship them. "Well," you say, "I don't even know what a graven image is, and if I did I'm sure I wouldn't bother with one." But have you ever bought a new house or a new car and been so pleased with it that you placed it above God? Have you ever bowed down in your heart before a movie star or a rock idol? Have you ever created a god in your heart that was not the God of the Bible, perhaps a god who makes no demands but promises to bless you? Have you ever thought that maybe, just maybe, there was power in a cross you hung around your neck or a rabbit's foot you carried in your pocket? Guilty!

The third commandment says we should never take the name of God in vain. "Well," you say, "I certainly don't swear." Maybe not, but have you ever promised God something you didn't deliver? Have you ever prayed a prayer or sung a hymn that you didn't mean? Have you ever portrayed yourself as a godly person without living as one? Guilty!

The fourth commandment says we are to keep and honor the Sabbath day. "Well," you say, "maybe I haven't always done that." As a matter of fact, it could be that you have violated this commandment more than you think. Do you set aside one day, twenty-four hours, a week for God? How about setting aside eight hours a week, or two, or one? Have you ever violated the body God gave you as a gift, by refusing to give your body rest? Have you ever decided that playing golf, going fishing, or sleeping was more important than the worship of God in the presence of His people? (Perhaps you've heard about the pastor who wanted to play golf on a Sunday morning. He got his associate to preach for him while he went out on the links. He had the best game of his life. In fact, he got three holes in one. When an angel expressed his dismay that God would reward the pastor in that way for his negligence, the Lord replied, "Don't you see, I have exacted the proper punishment: Three holes in one, and he won't be able to tell a single soul!") Have you ever profaned God's day with your profane actions? Guilty!

The fifth commandment says we are to honor our fathers and mothers. Think about the way you have treated your parents. Think about the times you were disobedient, made fun of their "old-fashioned" ways, or talked about them behind their backs. Have you turned away from the values taught by your mother or father? Have you ever been ashamed of them? Have you ever felt burdened by the emotional baggage placed on you by your parents? Guilty!

The sixth commandment says we should not kill (literally, *murder*). "Well," you say, "I'm certainly no murderer." Perhaps you have never killed anyone with a knife or a gun, but have you ever killed someone with your words? Have you ever been the causative factor in someone's turning away from God? Have you ever ignored a brother or a sister, laughed at his efforts or criticized her ways? Have you ever been the person who created the loneliness in another's heart or promoted sin in another's life? Have you ever failed to give witness of the gospel of Christ? Have you ever remained silent in the face of hunger, racism, or oppression? Have you ever looked at a hungry, frightened, desperate world and turned away? Guilty!

The seventh commandment instructs us not to commit adul-

tery. Jesus said in Matthew 5:27–28 that the seventh commandment prohibits more than sexual intercourse; lust is adulterous,
too. Have you ever desired a sexual relationship with someone
other than your husband or wife? Have you ever wondered
what it would be like to cheat a little? Have you ever fantasized
or dreamed about an adulterous relationship? In his *Confessions*,
Augustine was frustrated by his memory of sexual sin. He cried
out, "Great is the power of memory, a fearfull thing, O my God,
a deep and boundless manifoldness; and this thing is the mind,
and this am I myself. What am I then, O my God?"[2] Have you
ever allowed your mind to wander through forbidden fields of
sexual fantasy? Guilty!

The eighth commandment teaches us not to steal. "At least,"
you say, "I'm no thief." No? Have you always been faithful to
God's requirements of stewardship? Have you always given your
financial assistance when you could afford it? Have you ever
used God's money for something else? A millionaire was giving
a testimony to a congregation about the importance of stewardship, and to inspire the troops, he told of an incident that happened when he was a boy. He said there was a missionary at his
church who was in desperate need of money. On that occasion
he had only fifty cents. It was all that he had in the world, but,
he said, "Moved by God's Spirit, when the offering plate came by
I put in that fifty cents. Ladies and gentlemen, I gave everything
I had." The man went back to his pew and sat down, where-
upon an elderly woman sitting behind him leaned over and said
in a stage whisper, "I dare you to do it again." Have you ever
sacrificed for God's work? Have you ever robbed God of the
time you ought to be giving Him, or of your talents? Guilty!

The ninth commandment says we should never bear false
witness against anyone. "I wouldn't do that," you say. Maybe.
Have you always been truthful in what you have said about oth-

---

2. Augustine, *The Confessions*, Great Books of the Western World, Robert Hutchins, ed.
(Chicago: Encyclopaedia Britannica, 1952), 78.

ers? Have you ever told only half the truth? Have you ever kept quiet when your brother or sister needed defending? Have you ever allowed an untruth to be told about another? Have you ever given someone the impression that you knew something you didn't know about another person? Guilty!

And then the final commandment of the Big Ten: God says we should not covet. Envy is wrong in the eyes of God. Only the very foolish or the very dishonest would not admit to the sin of envy. It's around us every day; it stares at us from our neighbors' garages; it glitters in the department store windows; it leaps up and laughs at us in the considerable gifts of our brothers' ministries. Envy haunts us at night when we try to sleep, telling us life is not fair.

The business community has another name for envy: They call it competitive motivation. There was once a rooster who went into the ostrich pen and got one of those gigantic eggs. He rolled it over to his pen, pushed it in front of the hens, and said, "Now, I don't want you to think I'm complaining, but I did want you to see what the competition is doing." Envy runs throughout the fabric of our lives. Guilty!

Of course we could spend considerable time talking about what God requires from us for the poor and oppressed; we could talk about how hard Jesus was on the sins of anger and pride; we could quote Paul on forgiveness, faithfulness, and love; we could speak of witnessing and evangelism, or integrity and honor. But if none of that makes the point, then maybe Jesus' words will make us see: "Therefore you are to be perfect, as your heavenly Father is perfect" (Matt. 5:48).

The bad news is this: You and I are sinners. We have enough selfishness and pride in our hearts to destroy all the good that is there. All the superficial and shallow talk about "self-image" and "moral perfectibility" will not change the fact that there is something seriously wrong at the very heart of things. There is something warped about human nature. James was not one to mince words. He said,

What is the source of quarrels and conflicts among you? Is not the source your pleasures that wage war in your members? You lust and do not have; so you commit murder. And you are envious and cannot obtain; so you fight and quarrel. You do not have because you do not ask. You ask and do not receive, because you ask with wrong motives, so that you may spend it on your pleasures. (James 4:1–3)

Sin's Effect

"All right," you say, "so I'm not such a good person. Big deal! I'm only human." I wish that were the only truth. Unfortunately, there is more to the bad news than what I've told you so far. Sin isn't just something you do that is human and makes no difference. Sin does things to you that conflict with the way you were created to be.

God doesn't sit in heaven and say, "Every time one of My creatures finds something interesting, fun, and exciting to do, I'm going to call it a sin, because I want to make My creatures miserable." Instead, God wants us to be obedient, so that we might live as fulfilled lives as possible. Benjamin Franklin was not known for his Christian commitment, but he spoke a biblical truth when he said, "Sin is not hurtful because it is forbidden, but it is forbidden because it is hurtful. Nor is duty beneficial because it is commanded, but it is commanded because it is beneficial."

It is important that we see what sin does to us. Have you ever blushed privately thinking about something you had done? Have you ever been robbed of sleep because your guilt was eating you alive? I heard recently about a young woman who said she knew she had become a Christian because of the bed sheets: Before she was a Christian they were always twisted and disheveled, but after she came to know Christ she would wake up in the morning with the sheets smooth and straight. She smiled and said, "I sleep better."

I think it was in one of A. J. Cronin's stories that a certain
doctor worked for one company for most of his career. He started out with high aspirations and a genuine desire to help people. But as the years went by, he sold his soul little by little. He
started drinking and became a self-centered, bitter man. His
wife died, and after her death he was going through her pocket-
book. He found letters from people he had helped and some
pictures of himself when he was a young, idealistic doctor. He
walked to a mirror, looked at the man he had become, and said,
"You thought you would get away with it, but, by God, you
didn't."

Sin does more than just hurt us; it also divides us from other
people. In your whole lifetime, you will be lucky if you have
three or four good friends. We have lots of acquaintances but
few friends, and do you know why? It's because we don't want
that many people to know what we are really like. You see, we
wear masks that hide the ugliness underneath. We show others
our masks so they won't see the way we really are. There are
only a few people who can see what is behind our masks and
love us anyway. So our sin separates us from other people.

By far the most horrible consequence of sin is that it separates us from our holy God. I used to have a dance band in high
school and college, and every time we played an engagement,
we closed with the song, "He." Perhaps you remember that
song; it said a lot of shallow and sweet things about God, and its
last line was that God always says, "I forgive." That sounds
good, but it just isn't true. God is not the kind of God portrayed
by the shallow folk-religion of our day. He is the God of the
universe who is holy and righteous. When He gives His commandments, He doesn't put them in the form of suggestions.
When He says, "The wages of sin is death," He means that those
who sin will be separated from Him eternally. Paul said, "To
those who are selfishly ambitious and do not obey the truth, but
obey unrighteousness, wrath and indignation [will be the
result]. There will be tribulation and distress for every soul

of man who does evil, of the Jew first and also of the Greek."
(Rom. 2:8–9)

It is very foolish to stand before the God of the universe and
be flippant about sin. Isaiah knew better. You will remember
that he was in the temple when he had a vision of God. He saw
the Lord on a high throne, with His train filling the temple. In
his vision, Isaiah saw heavenly beings surrounding God's throne,
and the beings were calling back and forth to one another, "Holy,
Holy, Holy, is the LORD of hosts, the whole earth is full of His
glory" (Isa. 6:3). Isaiah didn't say, "Wow! Isn't that something!"
He didn't say, "What a loving God!" He didn't say, "It is nice to
have a personal encounter in my heart with a wonderful God."
This is what he said: "Woe is me, for I am ruined! Because I am
a man of unclean lips, and I live among a people of unclean lips;
for my eyes have seen the King, the LORD of hosts." (Isa. 6:5)

One of the reasons most people are miserable is that they
were created to be in fellowship with their Creator yet they live
outside Him. Augustine said, "Thou hast created us for Thyself,
and our hearts are restless until they find their rest in Thee."
Pascal said that we have a God-shaped vacuum in our hearts,
and nothing fits in the vacuum except God. The problem is that
our sin separates us from Him. He is infinite and we are finite;
He is in heaven and we are on earth; He is holy and we are sinful. Our approach to the source of our joy, power, and forgiveness in God is blocked by sin. Don't let anyone tell you other-
wise. Paul cried out, "Wretched man that I am! Who will set
me free from the body of this death?" (Rom. 7:24)

The Bible says that at the fall of Adam in the Garden, a terrible disease entered into the world (see Rom. 5:12). It is a disease far more destructive than cancer, and it is universal. We sin
because it has diseased us; it is in our blood. We sin because
Adam sinned, but we also sin *as* Adam sinned. Almost all sin is
first degree sin, in that we contemplate it and play with it long
before we make it an active part of our lives.

And even when we understand the origin of our sin, we still

sin. Even when we understand that what we are doing is hurting us, we do it again and again.

The Good News

Now let's talk about the good news. The Bible says, "For while we were still helpless, at the right time Christ died for the ungodly [that's everybody]. For one will hardly die for a righteous man; though perhaps for the good man someone would dare even to die. But God demonstrates His own love toward us, in that while we were yet sinners, Christ died for us." (Rom. 5:6–8)

Most of us have a superficial view of forgiveness. Forgiveness is a simple thing, right? Wrong. Forgiveness is very difficult, because whenever anyone is forgiven, someone gets hurt. Think about it for a moment. If I punch you in the nose, you can choose to forgive me or not. If you choose not to forgive me, you can punch me back and things will be balanced out. But if you decide to forgive me, it's going to cost you that punch in the nose. There is no such thing as cheap forgiveness—on our part or on God's part. Forgiveness always costs.

Our being forgiven cost God His Son. Jesus bore the cost of our sin on the Cross. Paul said, "Therefore having been justified by faith, we have peace with God through our Lord Jesus Christ" (Rom. 5:1). That means you don't have to be guilty anymore. The relationship between you and God can be restored. You don't have to worry about bad self-image or death or hell. You can be totally, wonderfully, joyfully accepted and forgiven. Gert Behanna said that when she got up from her knees after confessing her sin before God and asking forgiveness because of Christ, she not only felt forgiven, she also felt *welcomed*.

The bad news is that we are sinners. The good news is this: If Jesus has come, we are forgiven. At the close of his life, John Newton said he could remember two things: "I am a great sinner

and Jesus is a great Saviour." That's true, and it is exciting. I'm
not okay, and you're not okay—but Jesus has made it okay.

Why We Don't Feel Forgiven

And then we have one final question with which we must
deal before bringing this subject to an end. If we are forgiven,
why do we still feel guilty? There are so many Christians who
have been forgiven who don't "feel" forgiven that it would be
wrong to pass them by. Day after day I listen to confessions by
Christians who ought not to be confessing. They have been carrying a burden of guilt for years, and they have been doing it
needlessly. If you are in that position, the rest of this chapter is
for you. If you still feel guilty when you ought not to feel guilty,
I want to suggest the three "R's" of release from false guilt.

First, let me suggest that you *readjust* your thinking. The
problem with many of us is that we have not truly understood
forgiveness from God's standpoint. When you became a Christian, you were reconciled to God through the blood of Christ.
The problem with many of us is that we see the reconciliation
only in terms of forgiveness for past sins. But when you became
a Christian you were made a child of God forever, not just until
you did something bad.

Most of us think of what Christ did for us in terms of a slate.
When we became Christians, God wiped the slate of our past
sins clean. Right? Wrong! When we became Christians, God
didn't just wipe the slate clean. *He threw it away.*

You see, it is not the sin that is important anymore; it is the
relationship, and the relationship is established forever. When
my children were born, I knew from the beginning that they
were going to be disobedient to me on occasions. I knew there
would be times when they would do wrong things. I knew they
would never be perfect. So I gave them up for adoption. Of
course I didn't! They are my children, and there's nothing they

can ever do to me or against me that will stop them from being my beloved children.

John 1:12 tells us that when we came to know Christ, we became children of the Father. That's settled, and we no longer need to try to earn God's favor. Confession for salvation never needs to take place again. Salvation is an established fact. Confession takes place only to keep the lines of communication open. Our feeling of guilt is often no more or less than our fear that if we do something bad, we will be kicked out of God's family. We falsely think that God is like an employer, teacher, or casual friend. He isn't. He is the Father, and fathers (at least good ones) don't stop being fathers. Comparing earthly fathers to the heavenly Father, Jesus said, "If you then, being evil, know how to give good gifts to your children, how much more shall your Father who is in heaven give what is good to those who ask Him!" (Matt. 7:11)

Second, not only should you readjust your thinking if you are suffering from false guilt, but you should also *reprogram* your mind. When I graduated from my quill pen and began writing on a computer, I learned about the occasional necessity of reprogramming. Christians have to do something like that with their minds. Let me explain. Most of us feel we are controlled by our emotions. We think that if we don't feel like doing something, we can't do it. We think that if our feelings suggest something to our minds, the feelings must reflect reality. If there ever was a lie, a real whopper, that's it. Let me give you a principle that can change your life: Your mind controls your emotions, and you control your mind. Feelings, emotions, and proclivities are not reality. Anyone who tells you different has lied to you.

As a pastor, I have performed hundreds of marriage ceremonies. Often newly married people say something like, "I don't feel married." And I often reply, "Stay with it a while. It takes a bit of getting used to. Eventually the truth will sink in."

Now let's suppose a newly married couple doesn't take my advice and their feelings are more real to them than the fact that they're now married. Let's suppose, further, that every time they suspect they're married, they say to themselves, I *can't be married because I don't feel married.* Believe it or not, they are programing their minds in a certain way. I suppose that if they pushed it far enough and often enough, they would never think they were really married. If someone asked them if they were married, they would always reply, "No, we're not married." After a while, their feelings would become reality.

That's what a lot of Christians have done with their feelings of sin. In 1 John 1:9 we read, "If we confess our sins, He is faithful and righteous to forgive us our sins and to cleanse us from all unrighteousness." That's a fact. If you have confessed your sins, you are forgiven. If you don't feel forgiven, you are doing what our imaginary couple has done. You have simply denied the facts for your feelings. Whenever you feel guilty about something you have confessed, reprogram your mind. Say to yourself, "I have confessed that before God; He is not a liar; He has told me that I'm forgiven; therefore, I am forgiven. Anything other than that fact is a lie, and I will treat it like any other lie. I won't believe it." Then ask God to give you the grace to treat it as a lie.

Is this a magic formula? Of course not. It's a part of a process whereby gradually you learn to live your life by the facts and not by emotions. One day you will wake up and say, "I'm free! Praise God almighty, I'm free!"

And then one final word. If you suffer from false guilt, not only should you readjust and reprogram, but you also should *review.* Suffering from false guilt is one of the most subtle ways in which Satan goes after Christians. It's not a problem you deal with once and then it's over. When you least expect it, you'll find you have fallen into the sin of false guilt. And so a Christian needs to review God's grace constantly and praise Him for it.

Yesterday my wife and I worshiped at a church where a friend of mine is the pastor. I had been feeling guilty about a number of things, and without my knowing it, was walking around bearing false guilt. When we entered the sanctuary, I noticed that my friend's sermon was going to be about sin and forgiveness. I thought to myself, I *wish he would talk about something else. I already know all the things he is going to say.* As a matter of fact, I did know all the things my friend would teach that morning. But do you know what happened? As my friend taught the old truths from the Scriptures, I found myself free. The Holy Spirit was once again applying the truth of Jesus and His love to my life. I left that church feeling like a new man.

No Christian knows the truth of God's grace so well that he or she doesn't have to hear it again and again. If you have a problem with false guilt, let me suggest that you review, memorize, and think about the great message of the Bible: You don't have to be guilty about the sin that Christ has already taken to the Cross. You are forgiven.

In *Prime Rib and Apple,* Jill Briscoe has a great description of Eve's eating the forbidden fruit in the Garden of Eden. "Prime Rib [Eve] took the hand Omnipotence [God] had fashioned from her little piece of bone and plucked the piece of forbidden fruit. She placed it between the lips Omnipotence had framed to praise Him and absorbed into her system the poisons of independence, selfishness, and death. *And Jesus prepared to leave for Bethlehem.*"[3]

---

3. Jill Briscoe, *Prime Rib and Apple* (Grand Rapids: Zondervan Publishing House, 1976), 19.

For Personal Insight or Group Discussion

1. What "bad news" must each of us accept about ourselves before we can hear the good news of the gospel? (Rom. 3:9-12, 1 John 1:8.) Do you agree with what you read in those verses?

2. How did you score on the "Big Ten"? Have you consistently kept any of the Ten Commandments? Which of them have you found most difficult to keep?

3. How has sin robbed you of your peace of mind? How has it affected your relationships with other people? How has it affected your relationship with God? (See Isa. 6:5.)

4. What is the good news, according to Romans 5:6–8? How does Paul, in Ephesians 1:7-8, express how good this news really is? How would you express it in your own words?

5. How should realizing that we are God's beloved children help us feel secure in His forgiveness?

6. How can the process of "review" help you remain secure in the fact that God has forgiven you? What specific items should this review include?

Seven

If Jesus has come . . .
I Have a Hero

If Jesus has come ...
I Have a Hero

For you have been called for this purpose, since Christ also suffered for you, leaving you an example for you to follow in His steps. (1 Peter 2:21)

A number of years ago, I was part of a committee that invited some two hundred pastors from all over the United States to the Los Angeles area. The purpose of the meeting was to bring together pastors from different denominations and backgrounds, with the hope that once they knew and trusted each other they would be able to unite against some of the problems facing our country. At one session we divided the pastors into small groups and asked each group to discuss two questions. The first question asked what the United States would be like if the whole country were permeated with the Spirit of Christ. The second question asked what we could do in our ministries to make that happen.

The answers to the questions were varied, but the most interesting response was to the second question. The topmost answer on every group's list was that our country has a desperate need for models of righteousness. In a world looking for heroes to worship, we need "heroes of righteousness." In other words, it is terribly important that the world see Christians as living examples of what we claim to believe. When the world asks, "What is love?" it ought to be able to look at Christians and find the answer. When people want to know what it means to care, to be involved, to understand, they ought to be able to look at the lives of Christians and find a definition for those terms.

The Power of Example

The proposition of this chapter is that we can become role models of righteousness because we ourselves have a perfect role model. Our role model, our hero of righteousness, is Jesus Christ. And to know Jesus, to know our hero, is to want to be like Him. A popular Christian song of several years ago had the refrain, "I've got a hero, Jesus is my hero, and I'll live every day for Him."

Heros inspire imitation. Jesus did more than that. He gave us a perfect example, and then clearly told us to follow that example. In John 13, Jesus gave a living illustration of service. He washed the disciples' feet and said, "You call Me Teacher and Lord; and you are right; for so I am. If I then, the Lord and the Teacher, washed your feet, you also ought to wash one another's feet. For I gave you an example that you also should do as I did to you" (John 13:13–15). In John 15:12, Jesus said, "This is My commandment, that you love one another, just as I have loved you."

Jesus came to die, but He also came to show *us* how to die; He came to love us, but He also came to show *us* how to love others; He came that we might be forgiven, but He also came that *we* might know how to forgive others. Jesus gave form to the idea of obedience.

I play golf. I'm not very good at it, but I'm getting better. My improvement has not come from reading books about golf. I've read many such books, and what they say sounds nice on paper. But when I put their tips into practice, they just don't work the way the books say they should. Instead, I have a friend who is an excellent golfer, and he has been taking me out on the course and giving me advice. Because he is showing me how to play better golf, I am playing better golf. The principle is this: An instruction plus illustration is better than just instruction.

That is what the incarnation is all about. We knew what to do, but now we know how to do it, because Jesus has shown us how.

Frustration in the Christian Life

I suspect that none of this is new to you. I suspect further that you have probably tried to follow Jesus' example for most of your Christian life but have had little success. After all, even if Jesus is your hero, you can't be expected to do everything He did. Right? Wrong! Jesus said, "Truly, truly, I say to you, he who believes in Me, the works that I do shall he do also; and greater works than these shall he do; because I go to the Father" (John 14:12). Jesus came to teach us how to walk in His ways *and do it successfully*.

If the thought of following Christ successfully frustrates you because you have tried so often and failed so miserably, let me welcome you to the club. There isn't a Christian alive who hasn't known that frustration—and I have felt it more than most.

It is my contention that Christians are frustrated in their obedience to Christ for two reasons. First, they are obedient to Him for the wrong reasons; and second, they misunderstand the example to which they are to be obedient. Let's deal with those problems in order.

Obedient for the Wrong Reasons

There are any number of wrong reasons for obeying our Lord. Many of us, for instance, try to be obedient to Christ in order to solicit God's love. In the last chapter, I spoke briefly about this problem, but now let's discuss it in more detail.

I have a friend who owns a candle factory. When I visited the factory I got an education in how candles are made. In this particular candle factory, the workers are paid on the basis of "piece work." That means they are paid according to how many units they turn out rather than how many hours they work. It was amazing to see how fast those folks could turn out the boxes of candles. They were moving so fast I could hardly see their hands.

Many of us think that piece work is the way we ought to relate to God. His love and blessings are meted out to us on the basis of our volume of production. Some Christians are moving about as fast as the workers in that candle factory. If we can turn out just one more prayer, one more evangelistic encounter, one more rally, one more dollar for the kingdom, one more loving act, then God will notice and He'll "up the pay."

Nothing, however, could be farther from the truth. In fact, that's the direction to total frustration. Let me remind you of 1 John 4:10: "In this is love, not that we loved God, but that He loved us and sent His Son to be the propitiation for our sins." God's love for us is not dependent on anything except God. His love isn't geared to our ability to earn it.

A man came into my study and said, "Pastor, if my daughter marries that idiot, I'm going to disown her!"

Now, to be perfectly honest with you, I didn't like the young man much more than he did, but pastors don't express those kinds of views. So I said to him, "Sit down, Bill. You don't mean that. You love your daughter, and whatever she does, your love for her shouldn't change."

One of the great doctrines of the Bible is called "the perseverance of the saints." The doctrine says that you don't hold God, but He holds you: Once you belong to Him you will always belong to Him, no matter what. The truth of that doctrine was one of the most wonderful discoveries of my life. I really wanted to please God, but I knew my own sin, and it scared me. So I held onto God until my knuckles were white. One day I just couldn't hold on any longer. I tried—I really tried, but I just couldn't do it anymore; so I let go, thinking I would fall into the abyss.

Do you know what happened? I didn't fall at all. In fact, I didn't even move. I found that He was holding onto me, and that was what really mattered. He told me, "I give eternal life to them, and they shall never perish; and no one shall snatch them out of My hand. My Father, who has given them to Me, is greater than all; and no one is able to snatch them out of the Father's hand." (John 10:28–29)

Paul was right:

Who shall separate us from the love of Christ? Shall tribulation, or distress, or persecution, or famine, or nakedness, or peril, or sword? . . . In all these things we overwhelmingly conquer through Him who loved us. For I am convinced that neither death, nor life, nor angels, nor principalities, nor things present, nor things to come, nor powers, nor height, nor depth, nor any other created thing, shall be able to separate us from the love of God, which is in Christ Jesus our Lord. (Rom. 8:35, 37–39)

If you are obedient because you want God to notice and love you, you not only are very frustrated, but you also are very foolish.

Second, a lot of Christians are obedient because they want to help God out with His world. One of the most interesting religious developments of the fifties and early sixties was the thought of Teilhard de Chardin, who mirrored the somewhat earlier philosophy of Alfred North Whitehead. Both men saw God as evolving with His creation: The creation is incomplete, just as God is incomplete. But hang on, God, we're here! We're working on it; we'll salvage the situation! And God reared back and gave a great, big, ol' belly laugh. (See Ps. 2:4.)

I don't know about you, but I'm tired of the feeling that everything depends on me. As a matter of fact, everything doesn't depend on me; everything depends on God, and He is perfectly capable of running His universe.

> Thine, O LORD, is the greatness and the power and the glory and the victory and the majesty, indeed everything that is in the heavens and the earth; Thine is the dominion, O LORD, and Thou dost exalt Thyself as head over all. Both riches and honor come from Thee, and Thou dost rule over all, and in Thy hand is power and might; and it lies in Thy hand to make great, and to strengthen everyone. Now therefore, our God, we thank Thee, and praise Thy glorious name. (1 Chron. 29:11–13)

Have you noticed the modern tendency to have systems? No matter what you want to do, you can find a system that will enable you to do it. You can find a book on how to have a happy life, how to pull your own strings, how to be number one, how to intimidate, how to build a house, how to get rid of ugly fat, and how to make a million without using any of your own money.

As we noted in an earlier chapter, Christians suffer from the same tendency. Someone has said that the chief end of man is to glorify God and organize Him forever. Implicit in the Christian systems—ten steps to knowing God's will; four ways to save your marriage; God's design for a better relationship with your children—is the idea that if we do them right, we will be helping God bring the world around to His way of thinking. Sometimes systems can be helpful to us, but when they become "helpful" to God, they smell like smoke because they are from the pit of hell.

Listen! God doesn't need any help. When your obedience is geared to that goal, it is not only frustrating—it is silly.

Third, many of us make an effort at obedience because we see God as some kind of monster who must be placated with our obedience. Of course, we would never say so, but we really feel it in our heart of hearts. In *Eternity in Their Hearts*, Don Richardson gives ample evidence to counter the spurious view that our concept of God developed from polytheism to monotheism and from primitive to sophisticated forms. He shows that almost all peoples began with the idea of one God, and that many of the primitive religions we study in high school and college are actually inferior forms of earlier, more accurate and sophisticated religions. Richardson tells the fascinating story of Ethiopia's Gedeo people. Deep in the hill country of south-central Ethiopia, the Gedeo tribe worships and sacrifices to a god by the name of Sheit'an. Sheit'an is an evil, malevolent god who demands sacrifices from his worshipers. While they sacrifice to Sheit'an, they are aware of, though rarely pray to, another god by the name of Magano. Albert Brant, a missionary to the Gedeo tribe, asked them, "How is it that you regard Magano with profound awe, yet sacrifice to Sheit'an?"

They replied, "We sacrifice to Sheit'an, not because we love him, but because we simply do not enjoy close enough ties with Magano to allow us to be done with Sheit'an."[1] Brant built on their understanding and taught them that "Magano's" son died to give them "close ties."

Are not Christians in the so-called developed nations often very much like the Gedeo people? We talk about the God of love who sent His Son to die on a cross in our place . . . yet we worship another god, who demands that we sacrifice far more than what has already been sacrificed in Christ. Our obedience

---

1. Don Richardson, *Eternity in Their Hearts* (Ventura, Calif.: Regal Books, 1978), 54.

comes from a need to placate this second god. We play Christian games in which we do a "bad" thing today, thinking that we're okay because tomorrow we'll do a "good" thing and the scales will be balanced. We are righteous and loving because if we aren't, the second god we worship will strike us with a lightning bolt. Obedience given to satisfy a monster god is like a sacrifice offered to the sun so that it will come up in the morning. Our frustration in trying to be obedient is magnified by such silly behavior.

The Right Reason to Obey

So why be obedient? *Obedience is the response of a child who has been loved.* Paul put it this way: "For the love of Christ controls us" (2 Cor. 5:14). Obedience is the natural response of the heart to the reality of love. Have you ever noticed how you want to please those who love you? My wife and I worked one summer after college with a camp for children. We had a group of four- to six-year-old boys in our cabin, and let me tell you, it was a growing experience. We learned lots of important lessons that summer (for example, don't feed little boys watermelon just before they go to bed!), but the best lesson we learned was how children respond to love. In this particular camp, we were not allowed to any kind of corporal punishment. We had to learn some ingenious methods of dealing with the children as well as with our own frustration.

Anna was a natural. She just loved those little boys until they would do anything for her. One boy, the meanest five year old of the bunch, did everything in his power to test her love. I will never forget the last day of camp when he brought a bouquet of wild flowers to Anna. With tears streaming down his cheeks, he said, "Miss Anna, I don't want to go home, because nobody there loves me."

Obedience is nothing more or less than the bouquet of flowers we give to someone who has loved us. Because God loves us, we can trust Him with our obedience, knowing that whatever He asks us to do will be for our good.

Jesus' Example Misunderstood

Christians are frustrated in their obedience because they obey Christ for the wrong reasons, and also because they have misunderstood Christ's example. Let's examine His example more closely.

Most of us think of Jesus' example as one of love, compassion, righteousness, and so on. There is some truth to that, but let me suggest that the real example Jesus gave us was not an example of action, but an example of *being*. That sounds kind of strange, so let me explain.

Jesus said, "If I do not do the works of my Father, do not believe Me; but if I do them, though you do not believe Me, believe the works, that you may know and understand that the Father is in Me, and I in the Father" (John 10:37–38). And again, "He who believes in Me does not believe in Me, but in Him who sent Me. And he who beholds Me beholds the One who sent Me." (John 12:44–45)

John made an amazing statement in the first chapter of his Gospel: "No man has seen God at any time; the only begotten God, who is in the bosom of the Father, He has explained Him." (John 1:18)

Jesus also said, "Truly, truly, I say to you, the Son can do nothing of Himself, unless it is something He sees the Father doing; for whatever the Father does, these things the Son also does in like manner. For the Father loves the Son, and shows Him all things that He Himself is doing" (John 5:19–20). In Jesus' "High Priestly Prayer," He prayed,

I do not ask in behalf of these alone, but for those also who

believe in Me through their word; that they may all be one;
even as Thou, Father, art in Me, and I in Thee, that they also
may be in Us; that the world may believe that Thou didst send
Me. And the glory which Thou hast given Me I have given to
them; that they may be one, just as We are one; I in them, and
Thou in Me, that they may be perfected in unity, that the
world may know that Thou didst send Me, and didst love
them, even as Thou didst love Me. (John 17:20–23)

Paul wrote, "He is the image of the invisible God, the first-
born of all creation." (Col. 1:15)

Do you see it? Jesus is our hero not primarily because of
what He did, but because of *who He was.* The example He set
was not primarily in His acting, but in His being. All the miracles of Jesus can be duplicated and sometimes surpassed by
God's servants in the Old Testament. Not only that, but He said
Himself that His followers would do greater works than He did
(see John 14:12). Nor was the principal impact of the incarnation in what Jesus taught. Everything Jesus taught can be found
in the Old Testament as well.

Nor was the primary impact of the incarnation of God in
Christ in His goodness. Of course, Jesus had to be the morally
perfect "lamb" in order to effect our salvation. But was it necessary that He provide an *example* of goodness? No, it was not.
As a matter of fact, there were lots of examples of goodness God
could have used. We read in 2 Kings 22:1–2 that, "Josiah was
eight years old when he became king, and he reigned thirty-one
years in Jerusalem. . . . And he did right in the sight of the
LORD and walked in the way of his father David, nor did he
turn aside to the right or to the left." If God had needed an
example of goodness, He could have used Josiah.

So what was the impact of the incarnation of God in Christ?
Listen carefully: *The primary impact of the incarnation of God in
Christ is the incarnation of God in Christ.* "The Son can do nothing
of Himself, unless it is something He sees the Father doing"

(John 5:19). "My teaching is not Mine, but His who sent Me" (John 7 :16). "Now is the Son of Man glorified, and God is glorified in Him" (John 13:31). Jesus was not obedient so that He could become the Son of God. Rather, He was the Son of God, and was thereby obedient. He was not faithful in order to be God incarnate. He was God incarnate, and was therefore faithful.

Several years ago, while attending a conference, I met a man with whom I instantly struck up a close friendship. In the few short days we were together, we became very dear friends. Between the time I met him and the time I went back to speak for the same conference two years later, my friend went home to be with the Lord. So I returned to the conference with a good deal of sadness, knowing my friend would not be there. After the first evening session, a young man came down the aisle of the church and asked if he could speak with me.

"Sure you can," I replied. "And by the way, I knew your father and I loved him."

The young man was amazed. "How did you know who I am?" he asked.

"Are you kidding?" I said. "You smile like your father, you walk like your father, you part your hair like your father, and you talk like your father. You couldn't be anybody else."

Now let me ask you something about that boy. Do you think he stood in front of the mirror each morning and practiced walking like his father? Of course not. Do you think he worked for hours to get his hair to part like his father's? Do you think he worked with a tape recorder until he could sound just like his father? Of course not. He walked, talked, and looked like his father simply because he was his father's son. He didn't have to imitate—he just had to be.

Jesus was His Father's Son. He didn't come to show us how to speak Hebrew or wear a beard. His example was being, not acting. I heard two Christians talking not too long ago, one older and mature and the other a new believer. The older Christian was berating the new Christian because she had gone to a dance. The "spiritually mature" woman ended her lecture with these words: "My dear, can you imagine Jesus' going to a dance?"

The young woman thought for a moment and then said without any rancor, "No, I can't. But I can't imagine Him flying in an airplane, either." Out of the mouth of babes! She was beginning to understand the example Jesus gave us. Jesus didn't come to act out a play where He made a point to act in certain ways. Jesus came simply to be who He was. His example was primarily one of being and not one of acting.

Following Jesus' Example

Now here comes the important part. The *Christian life*, following Christ's example, is not so much a life of acting, but of being. Christians are called to abide in Christ in exactly the same way Christ abides in the Father. Jesus said, "Abide in Me, and I in you. As the branch cannot bear fruit of itself, unless it abides in the vine, so neither can you, unless you abide in Me. I am the vine, you are the branches; he who abides in Me, and I in him, he bears much fruit; for apart from Me you can do nothing" (John 15:4–5). Remember Christ's prayer in John 17: "I do not ask in behalf of these alone, but for those also who believe in Me through their word; that they may all be one; even as Thou, Father, art in Me, and I in Thee, that they also may be in Us" (verses 20–21). The example of Jesus calls us to abide in Him, as He is abiding in the Father.

"What a strange-looking cow," said the man from the city to his farmer cousin. "Why doesn't that cow have any horns?"

"Well, you see," explained the country boy, "some cows are born without horns and never had any; and others shed theirs; and some we dehorn; and some breeds aren't supposed to have horns at all. There are lots of reasons why some cows ain't got horns. But the reason that cow ain't got horns is that it ain't a cow, it's a horse."

There are lots of Christians who are trying their best to follow the example of Christ their hero. And do you know the result? They are simply tired. They are like horses trying to pretend they're cows. It has been said so many times that it has become a cliché, but it said so often because it's true: The Christian life isn't difficult, it is impossible. It has been perfectly lived by only one person, and that person is Jesus Christ. If you can live the Christian life at all, it is only because Jesus Christ lives it through you.

It is amazing to me the length to which Christians will go to get away from the simplicity of abiding in Christ. When their Christian lives have lost their power, they go to conferences on how to have spiritual power. When they feel that they are not experiencing normal Christian lives, they start reading the Bible a little more, praying a little more, and going to church one more time each week, thinking everything will be fine. Well, it won't be fine; and it won't be because that is not the way God ordained for us to walk with Him.

So often I have felt what John Michael Talbot expresses in his spiritual journal, *Changes*:

> I am wearied by a fellowship of many words. I grow tired of talking about the worship. I would much rather simply worship. I grow tired of talking about music. I would much rather simply make music. I grow tired of talking about humility and love. I would rather simply serve in humility and love. I grow tired of talking about "being" a Christian. I would much rather just "be."[2]

In one of his great classics, *The Pursuit of God*, A. W. Tozer made the same point:

> Every age has its own characteristics. Right now we are in an

---

2. John Michael Talbot, *Changes, a Spiritual Journal* (New York: Crossroad, 1984), 60.

age of religious complexity. The simplicity which is in Christ is rarely found among us. In its stead are programs, methods, organizations and a world of nervous activities which occupy time and attention but can never satisfy the longing of the heart. The shallowness of our inner experience, the hollowness of our worship, and that servile imitation of the world which marks our promotional methods all testify that we, in this day, know God only imperfectly, and the peace of God scarcely at all.[3]

If you want to be obedient to God, abide in Christ. Don't go on a pilgrimage to the Holy Land; don't do something religious like getting baptized in water shipped directly from the Jordan River; and don't wear another religious trinket or read another religious book (except, of course, this one!). Listen, if you want to be obedient to God, get close to Jesus. The Bible says, "This is the work of God, that you believe in [cleave to, trust, rely on, have faith in, lean on] Him whom He has sent" (John 6:29).

Now, if you are like me and most Christians, you want me to give you a system whereby you can abide in Christ. But systems are for computers, not people. In a moment I'll suggest some principles for abiding in Christ, but knowing Christ and abiding in Him doesn't require a system any more than knowing and abiding in your wife or your friend. The Greek word for *abide* means . . . abide! To abide in Christ is simply to stay close to Him, through His Word and His presence. It means you have to give time to the effort. It means you have to exclude other things. It means you simply have to stay close to Him.

Principle No. 1: Abiding in Christ is an act of faith. Paul said, "As you therefore have received Christ Jesus the Lord, so walk in him" (Col. 2:6). How did you receive Christ? You did it by faith. You knew you were a sinner, someone told you about Him, and you rejoiced in the good news that He would accept

---

3. A. W. Tozer, *The Pursuit of God* (Wheaton, Ill.: Tyndale House, 1982), 17–18.

you on the basis of His vicarious death on the Cross. Paul said that in the same way you received Him, you must walk in Him. How? By faith.

Let me suggest a prayer for you to pray, perhaps similar to the one you prayed when you became a Christian: "Father, You have told me that I am to abide in Christ. You made it a commandment, and therefore I know it is Your will that I abide in Him. Grant me the grace to follow Your will, and I accept in faith that I now abide in Him." That prayer is an expression of faith in the fact that you abide in Christ.

Principle No. 2: Abiding in Christ involves time. We want everything yesterday. Someone told me recently of a cartoon in which a cannibal was shaking the contents of a box into a boiling pot. The box was labeled, "Instant Missionary." We want everything instantly, and hardly anything worth anything comes instantly. It took time for you to develop your really close friendships. A good marriage doesn't just happen after you say "I do." A good marriage takes years to develop. The same is true for a relationship with Christ.

Principle No. 3: Abiding in Christ involves utilizing the means of grace He has given. You can't abide with someone without talking to him, listening to him, or being a friend to his friends. Prayer, Scripture reading, and fellowship with other Christians are essential tools for being with Christ.

Principle No. 4: Abiding in Christ means just being with Him. I have a tendency to think that reality is found in what I do; so my prayer life tends to be more doing than anything else. I pray for two or three hundred people each morning, and when I finish praying for them and start talking to Christ, I usually just "blither" before Him. Sometimes I feel He is saying to me, "Just be quiet. Just stop talking. Just be quiet for a change and let's be together." I am learning to do that, and the more I just silently meditate on His Person, His love, and His grace, the more I become like Him.

Someone has said that hurry isn't from the devil, hurry *is* the devil. That's very true in my life. I need to stop doing things and start just being with the One who (much to my amazement) wants just to be with me. I believe Christ would like to speak to us in the silence, but we are so busy talking and doing that we can never hear Him. Someone tells about an archbishop who went to the cathedral to have his evening devotions. He knelt before the chancel steps and prayed in a loud voice, "O Lord Christ."

A voice echoed from heaven, "Yes, child."

They found the archbishop the next morning dead from a heart attack. We ought to be surprised when God *doesn't* speak, not when He does.

We don't need to grow in order to abide in Christ; growth comes from abiding in Him. That's why so many of us are so frustrated in our walk with Christ. A dog doesn't bark to become a dog; a dog barks because he is a dog. Just so, a Christian doesn't do good things in order to be a Christian. A Christian does good things because he is a Christian. Stay close to Christ, and you will be surprised at the growth you'll experience. His gift to you for just being with Him is that you will become more and more like Him. Love, joy, peace, patience, kindness, goodness, faithfulness, gentleness, and self-control (see Gal. 5:22) are not the things you do in order to abide in Christ's Spirit. They are the fruit that comes *from* abiding in Christ's Spirit.

When Charles Kingsley was asked the secret of his productive life, he didn't write a book on how to be successful. He simply smiled and, referring to F. D. Maurice, said, "I had a friend." That's it. That's the secret, and you should not let its simplicity fool you. Obedience has form, and that form is Jesus Christ. When people see what He has done in your life, simply smile and say, "I have a hero; and He's also my friend, who loves me and will love me forever."

For Personal Insight or Group Discussion

1. What public figures or personal acquaintances have you looked up to as "heroes"? Are any of them still your heroes today?

2. Have you ever thought of Jesus as your hero? What things about Jesus would you most like to imitate in your own life? What things about Him do you find the most difficult to imitate?

3. Do you see any relationship between seeing Jesus as your hero, and wanting to live a life of obedience to Him?

4. How does the image of the vine and the branches (John 15:4–5) express the right reason for obedience? What does it mean to "abide" in Christ?

5. Do you agree that "abiding in Christ involves time"? What changes are needed in your life to give you time enough to abide in Christ?

6. How should the truths expressed in John 10:28–29 and Romans 8:35, 37–39 affect your attitude about being obedient to God?

Eight

If Jesus has come . . .
I'll Share in His Victory

If Jesus has come...
I'll Share in His Victory

For He delivered us from the domain of darkness, and transferred us to the kingdom of His beloved Son. (Colossians 1:13)

I'm writing these words the morning after the night before. The Republican National Convention ended last night, and now that both major political parties in the United States have finished their conventions, the campaign will swing into high gear. I watched both the Democratic and Republican conventions on television, and found myself having very strong feelings about many of the issues addressed by both parties. There were times when I felt proud to be an American, and other times when I was ashamed. I cheered my candidates, thrilled to their speeches, and winced when a reporter said something negative about them. I found myself so involved with the political speeches and debates that I fell into the trap of thinking the outcome of the world depended on the outcome of the election. I was so emotionally involved that I found myself thinking, *If so-and-so is not elected, our country is in terrible trouble. In fact, given the positions taken by the other candidate, I wonder if we would even survive.*

But now it is the morning after the night before, and I'm feeling better. I might even get well. This morning, after all the politics, I'm thinking like a Christian again, and I have remembered the truth that God is sovereign and is in charge. I've remembered the truth about the political parties, the speeches, the flags, the noise, the promises, the institutions, the money, the hype. It's all going to pass away, and none of it will be of any use except as the God of the universe decides to use it. It's sort of like watching an old movie on television when you realize that everyone who played in it is dead. The ultimate fate of the United States and the whole world is not dependent on the Republicans or the Democrats, the communists or the capitalists, the conservatives or the liberals. The ultimate fate of the world is dependent on God.

When the former Archbishop of Canterbury, Geoffrey Fisher, visited Jerusalem, he accomplished what was almost impossible: He received the unanimous praise of all the religious factions in the Holy City. As if that were not enough, he then went to Istanbul, where he received a royal welcome from the Ecumenical Patriarch. From there Fisher went to Rome, where he was received with open arms by Pope John. Then Archbishop Fisher returned home, where he was met by a crowd of reporters.

One of the reporters asked the Archbishop what his most memorable experience was while on his history-making journey. He thought for a moment and said, "My most memorable experience was of a camel that looked at me with ineffable scorn." Maybe that camel knew something others had forgotten: "Remember Him before the silver cord is broken and the golden bowl is crushed, the pitcher by the well is shattered and the wheel at the cistern is crushed; then the dust will return to the earth as it was, and the spirit will return to God who gave it. 'Vanity of vanities,' says the Preacher, 'all is vanity!'" (Eccl. 12:6–8)

Have you ever noticed that history has a way of reversing the decisions and observations of the present? Our problem is that we make value judgments on the basis of incomplete data, and thus we place too much value on political elections and ecclesiastical journeys. I'm not saying, of course, that these things are unimportant, but perhaps the camel had the right idea. Perhaps this year's election and the unity of the religious leaders won't even be footnotes in the history books of the future.

If you had been present at the trial of Jesus before Pilate, the Roman procurator of Judea, Samaria, and Idumea, you would not have bet a nickel on Jesus of Nazareth. He was standing trial before the real power brokers of the world. The ecclesiastical power of the priests, the political power of the procurator, and the military power of the soldiers all seemed formidable compared to the wandering carpenter from Nazareth. But history has reversed the judgment and we know the truth: Nobody would even know about Pilate, the priests, or the soldiers had they not had their encounter with the carpenter.

It was an interesting trial. If you had been there, the words of Jesus would have seemed like the delusions of a deranged mind. As Pilate faced the carpenter, a cynical smile crossed his face and he stifled a yawn. He asked Jesus if He really was the king of the Jews:

> Jesus answered, "Are you saying this on your own initiative, or did others tell you about Me?" Pilate answered, "I am not a Jew, am I? Your own nation and the chief priests delivered You up to me; what have You done?" Jesus answered, "My kingdom is not of this world. If My kingdom were of this world, then My servants would be fighting, that I might not be delivered up to the Jews; but as it is, My kingdom is not of this realm." Pilate therefore said to Him, "So You are a king?" Jesus answered, "You say correctly that I am a king. For this I have been born, and for this I have come into the world, to bear witness to the truth. Everyone who is of the truth hears My voice." (John 18:34–37)

And so the claim was made. Was this a first-century Don Quixote? Maybe so and maybe not; nevertheless, the claim was there for all to hear and to decide.

The Choice

Apparently Pilate had started a custom on the Passover of releasing one political prisoner to the people as a gesture of benevolence. On this occasion, he offered a choice: Jesus or Barabbas. The Scripture says in Luke 23:19 that Barabbas had been thrown in prison for a civil insurrection and for murder. But the crowd chose Barabbas over Jesus.

Let me tell you something I'll bet you didn't know about Barabbas. His name was possibly a messianic title—*Bar* meaning "son of" and *Abbas* meaning "the father." There is a tradition that says Barabbas's given name was Jesus. Thus you have a man named Jesus Barabbas. And then note the way Pilate refers to Jesus in Matthew 27:22: "Then what shall I do with Jesus *who is called Christ?*" Why add "who is called" unless there was another Jesus present?

Some scholars believe Barabbas was one of a number of false messiahs who were in Jerusalem and its environs during the time of Jesus. Looking to the prophecies of the Old Testament referring to a military and political leader, Barabbas's leadership was one of violence, force, manipulation, and intimidation. Jesus' leadership was one of meekness, love, gentleness, and persuasion. Pilate gave the crowd a choice between Jesus Barabbas and Jesus Christ, and they chose the former because Barabbas understood the political realities of the world.

Almost two thousand years have come and gone, and people are still faced with that choice. We choose between Jesus Barabbas and Jesus Christ. They can't both be king; one is right and one is wrong. And most people are still choosing Jesus Barabbas because they honestly can't see the reality of the kingdom ruled by Jesus Christ.

I have a friend who says that every time the government hugs the church, the church hugs back. He's right, and that fact worries me, because when you embrace the ways of Barabbas's kingdom—when you use the language of Barabbas's kingdom;

when you learn the techniques of Barabbas's kingdom; when you accept the rewards of Barabbas's kingdom; and when you nod too much in the direction of Barabbas's kingdom—you are a part of Barabbas's kingdom. (If it walks like a duck, quacks like a duck, and looks like a duck, it probably is a duck.)

Jesus said, "Enter by the narrow gate; for the gate is wide, and the way is broad that leads to destruction, and many are those who enter by it. For the gate is small, and the way is narrow that leads to life, and few are those who find it." (Matt. 7:13–14). The kingdom of Jesus is not always popular. Sometimes it seems to be lost in the shuffle, but it is the only kingdom of any importance, and in the end, when God turns the last page of history, the announcement will be made: "Now the salvation, and the power, and the kingdom of our God and the authority of His Christ have come." (Rev. 12:10)

When Rome was finally invaded in A.D. 410, some Romans tried to blame the Christians. It was a natural, though spurious, accusation given the fact that Emperor Theodosius had made Christianity the official state religion. Fifteen years after his death, Rome fell, adding fuel to the contention that Christians were somehow responsible. Augustine was brought into the controversy through some correspondence with two Roman officials about the relationship between the church and Rome. Out of those reflections, he wrote *The City of God.* The opening section of that work is bold in its assertions:

> The glorious city of God is my theme in this work, which you, my dearest son Marcellinus, suggested, and which is due to you by my promise. I have undertaken its defense against those who prefer their own gods to the Founder of this city— a city surpassing glorious, whether we view it as it still lives by faith in this fleeting course of time, and sojourns as a stranger in the midst of the ungodly, or as it shall dwell in the fixed stability of its eternal seat, which it now with patience waits for, expecting until "righteousness shall return to judgment" and it

obtain, by virtue of its excellence, final victory and perfect peace.[1]

The Kingdom of God

The biblical doctrine of the kingdom of God is fraught with theological controversy. Although the purpose of this book is not to resolve it (even if I could), there are many questions about the kingdom of God about which Christians are in wide agreement. Let it be sufficient to say in passing that the kingdom of God has two realities, one in the present and another in the future. Paul said, "For He delivered us from the domain of darkness, and transferred us to the kingdom of His beloved Son" (Col. 1:13). That is the present reality, and if you are a Christian you are a part of the present kingdom of God. Jesus also said that when we pray we should pray, "Father, hallowed be Thy name. Thy kingdom come . . ." (Luke 11:2). That is the future reality of God's kingdom, and if you are a Christian you will continue to be a part of it then.

Now let me give you some facts that you ought to remember when you are deciding between the kingdom of Barabbas and the kingdom of Jesus. When Jesus came, we had an opportunity to see Him either as a wandering Nazarene carpenter or as the King. If Jesus was only a carpenter, then Jesus Barabbas's kingdom is the only legitimate one. Sometimes it will succeed and sometimes it will fail, but it is the only kingdom. On the other hand, if Jesus was the King, then your knee should be bowing before Him at this very moment. Consider the following facts, and you will never be able to say that nobody told you.

Fact No. 1: The kingdom's beginning was small. Jesus said in Matthew 13:31–32, "The kingdom of heaven is like a mustard seed, which a man took and sowed in his field; and this is smaller than all other seeds; but when it is full grown, it is larger than

---

1. Augustine, *The City of God*, Great Books of the Western World, vol. 18, Robert Hutchins, ed. (Chicago: Encyclopaedia Britannica, 1952), 129.

the garden plants, and becomes a tree, so that the birds of the air come and nest in its branches."

People often make the mistake of despising small beginnings. The works of Christ's kingdom have always had small beginnings. Christ is King of the Jews, and they started small. Nobody will deny that Abraham was a small beginning.

> Now the LORD said to Abram, "Go forth from your country, and from your relatives and from your father's house, to the land which I will show you; and I will make you a great nation, and I will bless you, and make your name great; and so you shall be a blessing; and I will bless those who bless you, and the one who curses you I will curse. And in you all the families of the earth shall be blessed." (Gen. 12:1–4)

Abraham was just a nobody God chose to use in creating the kingdom. You wouldn't have chosen him in a million years— but be careful that you don't despise small beginnings.

Bethlehem was a small beginning. Who would have thought that the King would come through Bethlehem? And the King's disciples? How would you like to have been on the personnel committee deciding on the King's court? Peter? James? John? Judas? You've got to be kidding! The kingdom had a small beginning, but don't let it fool you.

To ensure that his son would be the heir of his kingdom, a king once required his nobles to swear allegiance to his son while he was only an infant. They laughed and refused, but the king changed their minds with these words: "Gentlemen, he is little now, but he *will* grow." Sometimes things of great import and worth begin very small—things as small and insignificant as a group of wandering Jews in the middle of the desert, a prophet from the hill country of Tekoa, or a carpenter behind a bench in Nazareth. Beware of small beginnings; they have a tendency to grow.

Fact No. 2: The kingdom's operation is often secret. You

don't ever see a mustard seed growing until it is out of the ground, and even then you might miss it. You turn around and say, "Wow, I never noticed that tree before." You see a tree's growth only in retrospect, by counting its rings.

I remember speaking at a missions conference for young people a number of years ago. I had a great sermon prepared on the mission enterprise of the church, but the leader came up to me right before I spoke and said, "Steve, we have just found out that a lot of these kids aren't Christians. Would you present the gospel?" So instead of making my missions presentation, I presented the plan of salvation and gave an invitation. Do you know what happened? Nothing. Not a soul stirred. I remember leaving the auditorium that night in shame. I could hardly wait to get on the airplane and head for home.

If you are a public speaker, you know how I felt. Every time I thought about that experience I blushed. I thought about how horribly I had presented Christ to those young people. I remembered my halting words and poor illustrations, and I just wanted to die. I tried to forget about it by saying to myself, *These things happen; no big deal.* But it *was* a big deal, and every time I heard the name of the town where I had given that presentation, I winced.

Let me tell you the rest of the story, however. Five years later, I was speaking at another conference, and a young man came up to me and said, "Mr. Brown, you don't know me, but a few years ago I was at a missions conference where you spoke." I thought, *Lord, what did I do to deserve this?* He went on: "The night you spoke, I received Christ, and now I'm a student in seminary and I'm going to be a pastor, and I just wanted to thank you. Not only that, but I've still got the tape of what you said that night, and I've shared it with my friends; I can't tell you how God has used your words." I thought, *Why didn't You tell me about this five years ago!* God was teaching me a lesson with that experience: You don't have to see the kingdom to get it to work. The kingdom operates in secret.

This is an important principle: If you have to "hype" your point, it probably isn't true or it isn't from God. Vance Havner said that Jesus performed miracles and didn't advertise, and we advertise miracles and don't perform them. He has a point. Most of the kingdom's important operations don't take place on television programs or in great crusades. They take place in people's hearts.

Don't underestimate the kingdom just because it operates in secret.

Fact No. 3: The kingdom's growth is slow. A mustard seed becomes a tree very slowly. I don't know about you, but I'm impatient. When you watch the kingdom grow, however, you have to be patient. The kingdom grows, but it grows slowly. Sometimes it even seems to retreat; sometimes it seems to lie fallow; sometimes you hardly even notice it growing. But don't be fooled. Slow growth is still growth, and Aesop was right about the tortoise and the hare.

When China was closed to missionaries, most Christians around the world were devastated. What would happen to the Christians in China? Could they stand the persecution? Would the church fall? I was in China recently, and do you know what has happened? The Christians who were left behind by the missionaries have multiplied at a phenomenal rate. When the Bamboo Curtain descended, there were about one million believers in all of China. C. Peter Wagner tells what then happened:

> The efforts made by the Communist government to extinguish the Church were massive. Pastors were jailed, Bibles were confiscated and burned, church buildings were closed, Bible schools were disbanded, Christian literature was outlawed, both lay leaders and clergy suffered humiliation, imprisonment, and torture, and most outside observers thought the Gang of Four and the Cultural Revolution would be successful in wiping out the Church. But as the bamboo curtain began to lift in the late seventies, and news began to filter out, it

became clear that the Holy Spirit had remained behind in
China and was doing mighty things. The first word was that
the 1 million were still there. Then the estimates continually
grew to 3 or 5 million, then 8 or 10 million and now even
conservative estimates range between 30 and 50 million.[2]

How about that? The story can be repeated all over the
world, from Africa to Korea, from India to Indonesia. On and
on the growth continues like a small hole in a dam, and then
another and another until there is no longer a barrier. Sometimes the missionaries wanted to go home, to throw in the
towel, to give up. But they didn't, because they knew about the
kingdom; they knew that God works by process; and when God
starts something, its slowness shouldn't be misjudged.

The Most Important Fact

I have given you these three facts first because I don't want
you to find yourself confused by the world's evaluation of success. The kingdom of Christ is small, secret, and slow. But it is
the kingdom of Christ—the Father gave it to Him (see Luke
22:29)—and His coming ensures that another fact, perhaps the
most important one, is also true: The kingdom's triumph is
inevitable. In the second chapter of Philippians, the apostle Paul
spoke of the amazing fact of the incarnation of God in Christ,
and then he said something no one should ever forget: "Therefore also God highly exalted Him, and bestowed on Him the
name which is above every name, that at the name of Jesus every
knee should bow, of those who are in heaven, and on earth, and
under the earth, and that every tongue should confess that Jesus
Christ is Lord, to the glory of God the Father." (Phil. 2:9–11)
    When you are choosing between the kingdoms of Jesus

---

2. C. Peter Wagner, *On the Crest of the Wave* (Ventura: Regal Books, 1983), 30.

Barabbas and Jesus Christ, remember that God has started something that can never be stopped. The kingdom has a King, and someday every knee will bow (the easy way or the hard way) and every tongue confess (the easy way or the hard way) that Jesus is the King.

Once I was flattered by an offer to pastor a very large church. I called a friend, the late Aiken Taylor, and asked him if I should consider the offer. Aiken was never one to hedge on what he thought, and he said, "Steve, are you crazy? That church is like a train. You don't change its direction, you just get on it!" The kingdom of Christ is just like that. You can watch the train go by, or you can get on it—but you can't stop it.

And someday, God will remove the option of getting on that train. The passenger list will be closed because the destination will have been reached.

Concerns of the King

There is still one more question to consider: What is the kingdom's destination? In other words, what is the King going to do? Where is He going? What is the ultimate result of the present reality of the kingdom? As one of the subjects of the kingdom of Christ, let me answer that by discussing four major concerns of the King.

Concern for His Glory

The King's first concern is for His glory and His Father's glory. In his high-priestly prayer, Jesus prayed two petitions that are of interest to this particular discussion. At the beginning of the prayer, He prayed, "Father, the hour has come; glorify Thy Son, that the Son may glorify Thee" (John 17:1). Then near the end of the prayer, He prayed, "Father, I desire that they also,

whom Thou hast given Me, be with Me where I am, in order that
they may behold My glory, which Thou hast given Me; for Thou
didst love Me before the foundation of the world." (John 17:24)

The Hebrew word for "glory" is *kabod*, translated *doxa* in the
Greek New Testament, from which we get the English word
doxology. The word literally means "to be heavy." It lends itself
to the idea that glory is laden with riches, power, position, and
worth. When a teenager says something is "heavy, man, heavy,"
he doesn't know it, but he's close to the biblical meaning of
glory. When Jesus talked about the kingdom's glory, He was
talking about the worth, praise, weight, dignity, power, and position it would receive.

Now the interesting thing in this context is that the whole reason for the creation of the world in general, and the creation of
you in particular, is that God would be glorified. "For from Him
and through Him and to Him are all things. To Him be the glory
forever. Amen" (Rom. 11:36). At the announcement of the birth
of the King, the multitude of angels praised God and said, "Glory
to God in the highest" (Luke 2:14). Paul wrote to the Ephesians,
"To Him be the glory in the church and in Christ Jesus to all generations forever and ever. Amen" (Eph. 3:21). In Luke 2:20, after
the shepherds beheld the Christ child, they returned home "glorifying and praising God." And then the culmination of the kingdom is coming, "And every created thing which is in heaven and
on the earth and under the earth and on the sea, and all things in
them, I heard saying, 'To Him who sits on the throne, and to the
Lamb, be blessing and honor and glory and dominion forever and
ever.' And the four living creatures kept saying, 'Amen.' And the
elders fell down and worshiped." (Rev. 5:13–14)

Do you see it? It's the purpose of the kingdom that the King
might be glorified. If you are looking forward to the future, that
is what you are going to be doing. If you want to be present at
the end, you will be praising the King.

In a very practical way, everything is more fulfilled and better
off when it is serving the purpose for which it was created.

I never asked them, but I suspect a tree is fulfilled in growing limbs and leaves, a cat is happy catching mice, and a dog is happy chasing mail carriers. You were created for the praise of the King's glory; and if you are not living a fulfilled and joyful life, you haven't found the secret: You can't glorify yourself and the King at the same time. The kingdom's purpose in its creation, its growth, and its end is that the King be glorified, and in His glorification His Son is glorified. Someday we are going to stand at the end of time, when the purpose of creation has been fulfilled, and we are going to look at Him and say to one another, "Isn't He something? Doesn't He shine? Isn't He wonderful?" Paul understood: "Whether, then, you eat or drink or whatever you do, do all to the glory of God." (1 Cor. 10:31)

Concern for His Subjects

You also ought to be aware of the King's concern for His subjects. Let me give you an amazing text: "So then let no one boast in men. For all things belong to you, whether Paul or Apollos or Cephas or the world or life or death or things present or things to come; all things belong to you, and you belong to Christ; and Christ belongs to God" (1 Cor. 3:21–23). Jesus said, "And you are those who have stood by Me in My trials; and just as My Father has granted Me a kingdom, I grant you that you may eat and drink at My table in My kingdom, and you will sit on thrones judging the twelve tribes of Israel" (Luke 22:28–30). Again Paul wrote, ". . . giving thanks to the Father, who has qualified us to share in the inheritance of the saints in light. For He delivered us from the domain of darkness, and transferred us to the kingdom of His beloved Son." (Col. 1:12–13)

In the kingdom's present reality, the King's subjects have His full interest and love. An ambassador for England once said, "I represent the greatest power on earth, and if I get into trouble it is that power that will stand with me." A Christian can say the same about the kingdom he represents. No wonder Paul said, "We are ambassadors for Christ" (2 Cor. 5:20) and was secure in that fact.

One time George Washington was coming from his headquarters on a cold, snowy day. Nobody noticed as he watched a corporal browbeat his men into building a breastwork of logs. They tried and tried, but each time one of the logs fell into the snow. At one point, when a heavy log fell, Washington ran up and pushed with them until the log was in place. Washington then turned to the corporal and said, "Why didn't you help your men?"

"I didn't help them because I am the corporal," he answered.

"Indeed," replied Washington, throwing open his greatcoat and showing his uniform, "I am only the commander-in-chief. The next time you have a log too heavy for your men to lift, you can send for me!"

In that respect, the King is like Washington. He is not just a King who reigns over His subjects from afar. He is a king who has come to share with us the hardship of the kingdom on earth. He is a companion King, and that is no small thing.

Concern for His Enemies

Third, the King is concerned for His enemies. Paul said, "While we were enemies, we were reconciled to God through the death of His Son" (Rom. 5:10). If you are the enemy of the King, His offer of amnesty and acceptance is still available. James Buswell depicts God's Kingdom as being in exile while its territory is occupied by an enemy. But he points out that this King is remaining in exile, not because of weakness, but to give his enemies the opportunity to become a part of his kingdom:

> In the sense of the loyal underground in time of war, believers are now said to be within the "kingdom" of Christ. There is this difference, of course, that in time of war the underground

exists as such only because of the weakness of the government of the rightful king. The fact that Christ is not now actively governing this world and enforcing His law in all human affairs, is not based upon any weakness whatsoever in His government or in His powers but is solely based upon His grace and His longsuffering.[3]

Jesus invites all who so desire to join His loyal underground.

However, with all of that being said, there is still more to be said. "Don't assume," said Queen Victoria to the Archbishop of Canterbury, "that because God does not balance His books every Thursday, that God does not balance His books." With all God's graciousness and love, the kingdom's open door should never cause anyone to presume. "Therefore having overlooked the times of ignorance, God is now declaring to men that all everywhere should repent, because He has fixed a day in which He will judge the world in righteousness through a Man whom He has appointed, having furnished proof to all men by raising Him from the dead" (Acts 17:30–31). Only a very foolish person fools around with a sovereign King.

C. S. Lewis wrote,

> Do not let us deceive ourselves. No possible complexity which we can give to our picture of the universe can hide us from God: There is no copse, no forest, no jungle thick enough to provide cover. We read in Revelation of Him that sat on the throne "from whose face the earth and heaven fled away." It may happen to any of us at any moment. In the twinkling of an eye, in a time too small to be measured, and in any place, all that seems to divide us from God can flee away, vanish leaving us naked before Him, like the first man, like the only man, as if nothing but He and I existed. And since that contact cannot be avoided for long, and since it means

---

3. James Oliver Buswell, *A Systematic Theology of the Christian Religion,* vol. 2, (Grand Rapids: Zondervan Publishing House, 1962), 347.

either bliss or horror, the business of life is to learn to like it. That is the first and great commandment.[4]

Now we have a choice of kingdoms to which we will belong. But the time will come when the opportunity to choose will be gone. It will be too late to plead mercy before the King.

Concern for His Ultimate Reign

Finally, you ought to note the King's concern for His ultimate reign. Jesus said,

> But immediately after the tribulation of those days the sun will be darkened, and the moon will not give its light, and the stars will fall from the sky, and the powers of the heavens will be shaken, and then the sign of the Son of Man will appear in the sky, and then all the tribes of earth will mourn, and they will see the Son of Man coming on the clouds of the sky with power and great glory. (Matt. 24:29–30)

Jesus has already been given all power and authority in the world (see Matt. 28:18), but because of His patience and kindness, His hand is restrained. Peter said, "The Lord is not slow about His promise, as some count slowness, but is patient toward you, not wishing for any to perish but for all to come to repentance. But the day of the Lord will come like a thief." (2 Peter 3:9–10)

Jesus said that the kingdom could be compared to a field in which a farmer had sowed good seed. While the farmer was asleep, an enemy came and sowed some weeds in the same field. When the seeds began to grow, the weeds were intermingled with the wheat and the field was a mess. When the slaves saw

---

4. C. S. Lewis, *God in the Dock* (Grand Rapids: William B. Eerdmans Publishing Company, 1970), 47.

what had happened, they told the farmer and suggested that they pull the weeds:

> But he said, "No; lest while you are gathering up the tares, you may root up the wheat with them. Allow both to grow together until the harvest; and in the time of the harvest I will say to the reapers, 'First gather up the tares and bind them in bundles to burn them up; but gather the wheat into my barn.'" (Matt. 13:29–30)

If I were not a subject of the King, I would be terribly afraid. But for those of us who serve the King, the kingdom's message is one of great joy and comfort. Malcolm Muggeridge wrote, "As Christians we know that here we have no continuing city, that crowns roll in the dust and every earthly kingdom must sometime flounder, whereas we acknowledge a king men did not crown and cannot dethrone, as we are citizens of a city of God they did not build and cannot destroy."[5]

Jesus told us to pray, "Thy kingdom come. Thy will be done, on earth as it is in heaven" (Matt. 6:10). Someday that prayer will be gloriously answered. Someday He will return. Someday the King will claim His total sovereign rule. ". . . the Lamb will overcome them, because He is Lord of lords and King of kings, and those who are with Him are the called and chosen and faithful." (Rev. 17:14)

Someday a trumpet will sound, and we who belong to the King will look up, and His ultimate reign will begin.

Those are the facts, and I have given them to you as honestly as I know how, so that you can choose between the kingdom of Jesus Barabbas and the kingdom of Jesus Christ. Whether or not you believe the facts, those facts remain the same.

Someone told me recently about two pastors who were con-

---

5. Malcolm Muggeridge, *The End of Christendom* (Grand Rapids: William B. Eerdmans Publishing Company, 1980), 52.

ducting a funeral together. One pastor was to read the Scripture
and lead a prayer, at which time the other pastor was to give the
eulogy. As the prayer was coming to a conclusion, the pastor
who was to give the eulogy realized he had left his notes in his
study two floors above the chapel where the funeral was taking
place. He slipped up behind the pastor who was praying and
whispered in his ear, "I'm leaving. Keep praying until I get
back." The prayer was one of the longest in the history of that
particular church, but eventually the pastor who had forgotten
his notes found them and returned to the pulpit to deliver a successful eulogy.

I have often thought about that humorous incident and the
pastor's words, "Keep praying until I get back." Jesus said the
same thing to us. He said, "I'll be back; you keep on praying
until I return. Stay faithful and keep on keeping on until I get
there." It's scary sometimes, because you don't know when He's
coming and you're not sure how much longer you can keep
on keeping on.

Don't worry. It won't be so long that you'll have to give up.
He promised. He said He'd be back. You can hang your hat on
that.

I just thought you ought to know.

For Personal Insight or Group Discussion

1. Jesus said that His kingdom is "not of this world" (John 18:34–37), and that we must "Enter by the narrow gate" (Matt. 7:13) in order to be a part of it. Do you find these truths borne out by your own experience as a follower of Christ?

2. Explain in your own words the various ways in which the kingdom of God is like a mustard seed. (Matthew 13:31–32) How does this relate to the idea of being a part of God's "loyal underground"?

3. Why is it so important for those who are a part of God's kingdom to glorify Him in this present life? (1 Cor. 10:31) Do you need to make any specific changes in your lifestyle order to more fully glorify Him?

4. Why does glorifying God lead to a more joyful and fulfilled life? (See Rev. 4:11, Acts 17: 28, Gen. 1:27, Eph. 1:4–12.)

5. What do the following Bible verses reveal about the eventual destiny of those who are a part of God's kingdom?

    Matthew 25:43
    John 14:2
    1 Corinthians 2:9
    Colossians 3:4
    Hebrews 11:16

Afterword

If Jesus has come . . .
History Makes Sense

I am the Alpha and the Omega, the first and the last, the beginning and the end. (Revelation 22:13)

In chapter 2 (and to various degrees, in all the other chapters) we dealt with the problem of finding personal meaning in life. But life cannot be meaningful except in the context of a meaningful world. In this afterword I want us to consider how Jesus Christ enables us to make sense of human history.

It is easy to be pessimistic about history. When you examine history in a superficial way, you can understand Edward Gibbon's comment, made after a lifetime of writing about it, that history is "little more than the crimes, follies, and misfortunes of mankind." If you are like me, you found history rather boring in high school and college. You memorized the names, the dates, and the battles, and gave them back to the teacher on the exam, then promptly forgot them all as irrelevant and unimportant. What could dead people possibly have to say to those of us still alive?

I'm a lot older now and a little wiser, and do you know what I have found? History isn't as dry as I thought it was. In fact, I have found that the things I think, believe, and appreciate are deeply rooted in the history of my culture. But more important than that, I have found that Christians simply cannot afford to avoid the lessons of history. More often than not, superficial Christians are people who have no sense of heritage and purpose, who never think about anything except how the Christian faith will make them happy and well.

I like to read C. S. Lewis's science fiction. It opens my mind to think of God as more than a nice deity who helps me with my mortgage payment. It allows me to see God as the God of the universe, whose power and greatness force me to stand in awe and wonder and praise. Little gods have little worshipers; and when big, bad things happen to little worshipers, they fall apart.

In order for Christians to stand against the lusty, materialistic paganism that is now running rampant across the world, we must have a world view that is as big as the God we worship. If we don't, we will be eaten alive. There is probably no better place for a Christian to develop a greater world view than in the study of history and God's part in it.

Now don't get me wrong. I have no vested interest in seeing you become a historian. I couldn't care less how many facts and dates you can recite. But I do want you to develop a view of history that will honor our God. I want Christians, myself included, to have a view of God that won't crumble when the first thoughtful nonbeliever utters an angry protest.

I am writing this in a friend's apartment that overlooks the ocean. Occasionally I look up from the typewriter and hear the crashing waves and look at the magnificent blue water. When I do, I remember the greatness and power of God. It helps when I go back to the typewriter. Just so, we Christians need sometimes to look up from the mundane (though necessary) activities of life. We need to look at a God who is greater than anything we can imagine. When we go back to the tasks of "just keeping on keeping on," we then will be refreshed with new meaning and purpose.

Some of what follows may seem difficult. But stay with me, because it is important.

The Subjectivity of History

We live in a time when Christians are questioning the secular humanism in the public school system. The questions being asked are good ones, but I would suggest we ask many more questions about our history books. Future generations will be affected far more by history than by science. Science books are old almost as soon as they are written. In fact, if you want to get your library down to size, throw away every science book you have that is more than ten years old. We don't throw away history books, because we have somehow come to the conclusion that a history book, no matter how old it is, is always good, because it is an objective record of past events.

There has never been an objective history book! Lucian, the Greek satirist of the second century A.D., said about the writing of history that, "Facts are not to be collected at haphazard, but with careful, laborious, repeated investigation." He went on to say, "History abhors the intrusion of any least scruple of falsehood; it is like the windpipe, which the doctors tell us will not tolerate a morsel of stray food." Now, Lucian sounds good until you read further and find that he recommended selectivity about the facts of history. In order to select properly, Lucian said, we need "political insight." And where can we get "political insight"? Lucian said it is a gift of nature that "can never be learned." As a matter of fact, the "political insight" about which Lucian spoke was nothing more or less than his own subjective philosophy of history.

History began to be written almost as soon as the appearance of writing itself. When you examine the records of Egypt, China, and Mesopotamia, you find that conquering kings wanted to record their successes for later generations to read. You could hardly expect those records, commissioned and paid for by egotistical kings, to be objective. The organizing principle of the history books was the public relations of the king. Some six thousand years later, things haven't changed in the writing of history as much as we might like to think. There is always an organizing principle or philosophical view that affects what is recorded.

I am not saying that there are no reliable facts in history books; nor am I saying that historians deliberately distort facts. There are both responsible and irresponsible historians, just as there are both responsible and irresponsible scientists, preachers, and secretaries. But the writing of history is not just the stringing together of facts. It involves two other important principles: *philosophy*, the historian's principle for organizing the historical data; and *selection*, the historian's principle for choosing from the vast data of history what he or she will record.

No historian goes to his task without some kind of philosophy, and that philosophy determines the "facts" he will use. The ancient view that history is cyclical, and the modern view that history is evolutionary, are both philosophies that have affected the writing of history. G. K. Chesterton's comment that Buddha is usually portrayed with his eyes closed because there is nothing important to see, lends insight to the Eastern view of history—that external events simply are unimportant. Hegel's idealism and Marx's materialism both require seeing history as an evolutionary movement. And then there are those modern historians who say that history has no meaning; and that assertion itself is their organizing principle.

The Bible's Philosophy of History

The Bible also has a philosophy of history. The Bible is not primarily a book of doctrine or of theology; it is the record of God's actions in history. The Bible proclaims from beginning to end that history is "His story." If you want to know what God has done in the past, read any history book, especially the Bible. If you want to know what God is doing right now, read the newspapers. And if you want to know what God is going to do in the future, read the Bible's prophecies.

The Bible is a history book, and like any other history book it has a philosophy of history, an organizing principle to explain the history it presents. That organizing principle is Jesus Christ. The Christian faith proclaims that the God who controls history has Himself become a part of the history He controls. He has interacted with history in a specific person, a Jew by the name of Jesus. Oscar Cullman suggested that the biblical view of history does not reckon time in a continuous succession of events moving forward from one point to another. Rather, he suggested, biblical history starts at the center, Jesus Christ, and moves backward and forward from that "Christ event." In his book *God and History*, James Montgomery Boice said, "The appearance of Jesus was the decisive intervention of God in history. It gave the conclusive meaning to history as well as the basis for judgment upon it."[1]

Paul clearly saw Christ as history's organizing principle when he wrote in Ephesians of, "the fulness of the times, that is, the summing up of all things in Christ" (1:10). And in his letter to the Romans, he showed how all of human history revolves around "the obedience of the One," through which "the many will be made righteous." (5:19)

Jesus Himself spoke of His central place in history. After His baptism by John, He said, "The time is fulfilled, and the kingdom of God is at hand." (Mark 1:15)

The New Testament proclaims the glad news that the world has received the God of history into time and space. The followers of Christ knew they had found the key to everything that had ever happened, that was happening, and that ever would happen in the world. Their organizing principle was absolute. Jesus of Nazareth is what history is all about.

In John 15:1, Jesus made an amazing statement. He said, "I am the true vine." His claim does not seem radical until you know its background. Jesus was not speaking in a vacuum. He

---

1. James Montgomery Boice, *God and History* (Downers Grove, Ill.: InterVarsity Press, 1981), 22.

was a Jew, speaking to Jews about a well-known Jewish concept. In Psalm 80 we read: "Thou didst remove a vine from Egypt; thou didst drive out the nations, and didst plant it. Thou didst clear the ground before it, and it took deep root and filled the land" (verses 8–9). "O God of hosts, turn again now, we beseech Thee; look down from heaven and see, and take care of this vine" (verse 14). Isaiah said, "For the vineyard of the LORD of hosts is the house of Israel, and the men of Judah His delightful plant" (Isa. 5:7). Jeremiah called Israel "a choice vine" (Jer. 2:21). Ezekiel (19:10) and Hosea (10:1) used the same image.

When Jesus said that *He* was the *true* vine, those passages would have come to the mind of His followers. Just as an eagle reminds Americans of their country, the vine reminded Jesus' Jewish listeners of *their* nation, Israel. During the Maccabean period, the coinage of Israel was imprinted with a vine, just as many of the coins of the United States bear an eagle. Jesus was saying, "I am the essence of the nation of Israel; I am the personification of everything Israel was created to be."

God is the Creator and sustainer of history. He started it; He will bring His purpose from it; and He will bring it to a close when that purpose is decided. But if you want to understand what God is doing in history, you have to look at Jesus. *He* is the explanation of God's words and actions throughout all of history. If you want to know what the church is to be like, look at Jesus. If you want to know where history is moving, look at Jesus. He is the organizing principle behind everything God ever intended to do in the world.

The Difference Jesus Make

So what difference does the Christ event make? First, if Jesus Christ is the organizing principle of history, we know something about history's *past*. We know that history is not just a series of events without meaning or purpose. History has been created by a Creator who has visited His creation.

This means that Christians should approach the study of history quite differently than nonbelievers approach it. As Herbert Schlossberg points out in his very good book, *Idols for Destruction*, they often fail to do so:

> The modern historical profession . . . . assumes that the expla-nation of history lies within itself. . . . What the historian is unable to explain must be a matter of defective or incomplete sources or of his own limitations in drawing inferences from them. His failure to acknowledge that the explanation of his-tory may lie outside of history is analogous to the naturalism of the physical and biological sciences, which also sees "the whole show" in the artifacts of creation. There is no evidence for this point of view, but being an assumption, it can live without evidence. The historians who hold it—most histori-ans, that is—would express bewilderment that it should seri-ously be questioned. Even those historians who explicitly dis-believe it—Christians, for example—write history as if they do believe it. They are stretching the necessarily artificial boundaries of an academic discipline to encompass all of reality, accepting assumptions as professionals that they do not accept as individuals.[2]

Christians, just like their nonbelieving friends, often try to find history's meaning within itself. But the writers of the Bible consistently looked beyond history for its meaning: Genesis declares, "In the beginning God created" (Gen. 1:1). The psalmist said, "Know that the LORD Himself is God; it is He who has made us, and not we ourselves" (Ps. 100:3). Again, "Of old Thou didst found the earth; and the heavens are the work of Thy hands." (Ps. 102:25)

As I was growing up I didn't care much about my family's "roots." But as I got older, my interest greatly increased. When

---

2. Herbert Schlossberg, *Idols for Destruction* (Nashville: Thomas Nelson, 1983), 23–24.

our father died, my brother and I started asking questions about
our background. We went to a number of towns in the mountains of North Carolina to talk to people who knew about our
family. We visited our grandmother's grave, and a country store
where our forefathers had worked. We walked across the land
where our relatives had walked, and we visited the little mountain school our father had attended. It had not been important
before, but when we realized that time was passing and that self-
identity is important, we began to check into ours. We asked the
older members of our family to tell us their memories, and we
traced our mountain relatives back as far as we possibly could.

Our feelings that evening were changed. We felt a sense of
satisfaction as we talked about our past and remembered the
hard-working mountain people who had given us the present.
We felt good about ourselves; we were able to define ourselves
and to claim an identity because of the knowledge of our past.

Knowing how history started should give the thoughtful
Christian similar feelings. History's Creator is God, and that
means that we are not animals or accidents of nature or dust.
We are creatures with a past, given to us by God. That is the
answer to the meaningless drivel that says all of history is darkness. Not so: The Creator has come to lay claim to His creation.
That's really good news.

A Christian historian can never see history as a meaningless
string of events. A Christian historian approaches his discipline
with reverence and prayer, because he knows he is engaged in
the study of God's hand as it molds, directs, and shapes history
for His own purposes.

Second, if Christ is the organizing principle of history, we
know something about the *present*: It is important. Throughout
the history of the Christian church, there have been those who
have tried to escape the reality of living. One Christian school
advertised that it was one hundred miles from any known sin,
reflecting a tendency among Christians that is neither biblical
nor helpful. It is the kind of attitude that suggests the world is

bad, bad, bad, and that Christians who are really Christians should always be trying to escape it.

One of the early Christian heresies was the heresy of Docetism (from the Greek word *dokeo*, meaning "to seem or to appear"). The Docetists taught that Jesus only appeared to be a real person. The Docetists taught that the world and the flesh were evil, and therefore it was unthinkable that Christ would really enter the world in human flesh.

That heresy has been floating around the church in one form or another ever since Marcion and the Gnostics first taught it. You will find it in the philosophy of the Desert Fathers, who could not abide the sinful world of human relationships and went into the desert to be alone with God. You will find it in the escapist songs that are still sung in the church. You can find it in the fundamentalism of those whose separatist views call them to go only to Christian movies, watch only Christian television, go only to Christian schools, eat only Christian cookies, and wear only Christian underwear. You can find it in the heart of a Christian man or woman who has no unbelieving friends, or in the superficial Christian thinker who believes that politics is somehow dirty and beneath the concern of the Christian.

When John said that the Word had "become flesh," he was once and forever making a statement about the importance and reality of the world. It is not beyond redemption; it is the focus of God's concern. It is the territory to which the Christian, following the footsteps of Jesus, is called. An uninvolved, uncaring Christian is a contradiction.

One of the problems with the Christian church is that it often becomes militarily defensible. We pull in our troops and raise the drawbridge. If we can just defend the castle,"they" won't get us. How different from the message of Jesus! After the confession of Peter, He said, "Upon this rock I will build My church; and the gates of Hades shall not overpower it" (Matt. 16:18). Have you ever been attacked by a gate? Jesus doesn't call us to retreat; He calls us to the battle for a world that is important. Our obedience should find expression in politics, in the arts, in education—in every area of the world—because Christ's coming has declared the world important.

Congressman Jack Kemp was once asked if a Christian could be a politician. He replied with another question, "Can a Christian *not* be a politician?" He had a point, and it was a biblical point. Present history must include the involvement of the Christian.

Finally, if Christ is the organizing principle of history, we know something about *future* history: It will end properly. I believe it was the historian Charles Beard who replied this way to the question of what he had learned from history: "I have learned that those whom the gods would destroy they first make mad; that the bee fertilizes the flower from which it robs; that when it is dark enough you can see the stars; and finally, I have learned that the mills of God grind slowly, but they grind exceedingly fine."

God is in charge of history; and because He created it and sustains it, history will come to a successful conclusion. Paul wrote to the Corinthians,

> Behold, I tell you a mystery; we shall not all sleep, but we shall all be changed, in a moment, in the twinkling of an eye, at the last trumpet; for the trumpet will sound, and the dead will be raised imperishable, and we shall be changed. For this perishable must put on the imperishable, and this mortal must put on immortality. But when this perishable will have put on the imperishable, and this mortal will have put on immortality, then will come about the saying that is written, "Death is swallowed up in victory. O death, where is your victory? O death, where is your sting?" The sting of death is sin, and the power of sin is the law; but thanks be to God, who gives us the victory through our Lord Jesus Christ. Therefore, my beloved brethren, be steadfast, immovable, always abounding in the work of the Lord, knowing that your toil is not in vain in the Lord. (1 Cor. 15:51–58)

After speaking about some of the signs of the end of the age, Jesus said, "And then the sign of the Son of Man will appear in the sky, and then all the tribes of the earth will mourn, and they will see the Son of Man coming on the clouds of the sky with power and great glory" (Matt. 24:30). After Jesus ascended into the heavens, an angel said to His disciples, "Men of Galilee, why do you stand looking into the sky? This Jesus, who has been taken up from you into heaven, will come in just the same way as you have watched Him go into heaven" (Acts 1:11). John wrote to the seven churches in Revelation, "Behold, He is coming with the clouds, and every eye will see Him, even those who pierced Him; and all the tribes of the earth will mourn over Him. Even so, Amen." (Rev. 1:7)

I do a lot of traveling from my home in Miami, Florida. If you live in Florida, the best time to travel north is during the winter. One of the great joys I have is speaking to a conference in the cold north where there is ice and snow. Even as I am speaking, I think, *As soon as this is over, I'm going back to where it's warm, where the palm trees sway in the breeze and the sun is shining.* A Christian views the future much like that. This world is a difficult place to serve; sometimes it requires hurt and suffering. It is a world that is important, a world much loved by God, but it can be a cold and bitter place. Our meaning, however, lies in the fact that Jesus has come. His coming pointed to the past, sanctified the present, and gave hope and meaning to the future. Jesus said, "These things I have spoken to you, that in Me you may have peace. In the world you have tribulation, but take courage; I have overcome the world." (John 16:33)

When the first steamship, the *Clermont,* was demonstrated, a great crowd of scoffers stood on the shore watching the strange craft trying to get up enough steam to move. Many in the crowd shouted, "She'll never start! She'll never start!" Nevertheless, to the astonishment of the scoffers, the boat began to move. But, after a moment of stunned silence, their cynicism simply changed words, as they shouted, "She'll never stop! She'll never stop!"

Some people scoff at the idea that time will actually come to an end when Christ returns. Peter spoke about this in his second letter:

> Know this first of all, that in the last days mockers will come with their mocking, following after their own lusts, and saying, "Where is the promise of His coming? For ever since the fathers fell asleep, all continues just as it was from the beginning of creation. . . . But the day of the Lord will come like a thief, in which the heavens will pass away with a roar and the elements will be destroyed with intense heat, and the earth and its works will be burned up. . . . But according to His promise we are looking for new heavens and a new earth, in which righteousness dwells. Therefore, beloved, since you look for these things, be diligent to be found by Him in peace, spotless and blameless. (2 Peter 3:3–4, 10, 13–14)

Just as Jesus helps us make sense of our past and our present, He gives us a future which we can hope for and work toward.

As we said at the outset, life cannot be meaningful except in the context of a meaningful world. Making sense of history is mandatory before you can make sense of your own life. When Jesus Christ is the organizing principle of history, you can realize the vastness of God's plan and, more importantly, you can see your own part in that plan as meaningful and important. As I think about history, and about God's oversight of history, I see my part as a piece of the puzzle. When it is completed, I will be a part of that completeness.

		DATE DUE		